Praises Abound

Praises Abound

Hymns and Meditations for Lent & Easter Week
from the Seminary of the Southwest

RUSSELL SCHULZ-WIDMAR, EDITOR

Church Publishing
NEW YORK

Unless otherwise noted, the Scripture quotations contained herein are from the New Revised Standard Version Bible, copyright © 1989 by the Division of Christian Education of the National Council of Churches of Christ in the U.S.A. Used by permission. All rights reserved.

Scripture quotations marked KJV are from the King James Version of the Bible.

Church Publishing, 445 Fifth Avenue, New York, NY 10016
www.churchpublishing.org

Cover design by Laurie Klein Westhafer
Typeset by Linda Brooks

Library of Congress Cataloging-in-Publication Data
Praises abound : hymns and meditations for Lent and Easter week from the Seminary of the Southwest / Russell Schulz-Widmar, editor.
    p. cm.
 Includes bibliographical references and indexes.
 ISBN 978-0-89869-867-1 (pbk.) — ISBN 978-0-89869-868-8 (ebook)
1. Lent—Meditations. 2. Easter—Meditations. 3. Lenten hymns. 4. Easter hymns. 5. Hymns—Devotional use. I. Schulz-Widmar, Russell. II. Episcopal Theological Seminary of the Southwest.

 BV85.P725 2012
 242'.34--dc23
                                2012012013

Printed in the United States of America

10 9 8 7 6 5 4 3 2 1

*My sincere thanks go to
Madelyn Hoffman and Aaron Hudson,
student assistants,
who helped bring this book together.*

Contents

Foreword

In the eighteenth and nineteenth centuries, on both sides of the Atlantic, many devout Christians kept two books on their bedside table. One was the Bible and, in the case of Anglicans and Episcopalians, the other was *The Book of Common Prayer*. Those whose convictions had led them to put aside the Prayer Book relied instead on the hymns they sang at worship week by week. Collections of hymns by Isaac Watts and later by John and Charles Wesley, among others, brought them comfort and inspiration. These much-loved texts, printed without music, were regularly read and reflected on, serving both as devotional material and as commentary on the Scriptures themselves.

For the most part Anglicans and Episcopalians lack that intimate familiarity with the hymns they sing week by week. Rarely do they encounter a hymn printed not with its musical setting but as poetry to be appreciated for itself. This has meant that, valued as the current Episcopal hymnal may be, it is an underused resource in the spiritual life and nurture of Episcopalians. In our pews hymns are sung with appreciation, even with fervor in some places, but in our homes the hymnal rarely occupies a place in our devotional reading and spiritual life akin to *The Book of Common Prayer*.

Fortunately, this situation is changing, and this collection of meditations and hymns written by students of Dr. Russell Schulz is encouraging evidence of the change. Meant to be read day by day over the course of Lent and then of Easter Week, this collection addresses themes that bear on our Christian journey in good times and bad. The death of a loved one, the grace-filled pain of reconciliation, the call to discipleship and holiness of life, the wonder of God's creation, the real-though-unseen presence of the saints and the growing nearness of the end of life—all find expression in these pages. Familiar hymns are mined for meaning in ways that we can affirm from our own experience, and new hymns give voice to what we find ourselves wanting to say and sing in private prayer and public worship.

"Morning has broken" (*The Hymnal 1982*: 8) inspired two of the meditations, one by a student whose son died at the age of seven and the other by a student whose grandmother was a devoted gardener. They could not be more dissimilar, but they both reflect engagingly on the familiar words of this hymn. "Taste and see" (*Wonder, Love and Praise*: 764) led a physician to reflect on the human body and the Body of Christ. The Good Friday hymn "Were you there when they crucified my Lord?" (*1982*: 172) moved one student to ask eleven further questions that will challenge the reader to set the sufferings of many of our neighbors alongside the sufferings of Christ on the Cross. And the meditation on the Easter hymn "Now the green blade riseth" (*1982*: 204) reminds readers, "The wind blows seeds and grain from field to field, from heart to heart the Love of God is sowed."

The new hymn texts will also be rewarding to reflect on as they provide memorable words and phrases to take with us on our way. "Dame Julian's Vision" begins its refrain with the words: "God holds the world, a hazelnut, and keeps us safe in hand." "Known only by our God" ends with a striking couplet: "Oblivion deposed! Our history composed!" A fine Trinitarian hymn, "Grace has kindled our desires," moves through the successive stages of the baptismal rite: "Death and Blessing in the water / Joy and Suffering in the water / Breath and Family in the water / Fire and Singing in the water." And the hymn "If I give up my voice today" asks poignantly, "Are you within this troubled world or are we all alone?" and the whispered answer comes back, "'My Word is written in the face of Jesus crucified.'"

Successive generations of students under the guidance of Dr. Schulz have been given an opportunity to prepare a meditation on an existing hymn or to write a new hymn text. Gathered here are some of the fruits of their labors. In so doing, these students have experienced firsthand what George Herbert said of those who look beyond the surface of things and see what lies within and beyond:

> A man that looks on glass,
> On it may stay his eye;
> Or if he pleaseth, through it pass,
> And then the heav'n espy.
> ("Teach me, my God and King")

May those who journey with this collection through Lent to Easter enter more deeply into the hymns we sing and with their help "then the heav'n espy." And in the words of one of the hymns in the collection, may we experience more richly the unshakable hope of Easter:

The widow cries, 'O Lord, how long?'
The bridegroom sings, 'Amen!'
God's listening breath sustains them both.
We die. We rise again.
    ("In winter's grip, the earth lies cold")

—JEFFERY ROWTHORN
Bishop in Europe (retired)
September 8, 2011

Introduction

Most of the hymns and meditations in this book were written over a period of thirty years by students in the liturgical music class at the Seminary of the Southwest in Austin. A few were written for different occasions or circumstances at the seminary. The class assignment was always the same: write an original hymn-text about something that is important to you, or write a meditation on a hymn that is meaningful to you. Each year, with students' permission, I made copies of a few pieces that were exemplary or representative or interesting for some reason.

Over the years, a rich collection drifted together. The variety was amazing: passionate and whimsical, lofty and casual, heartwarming and heartwrenching, questioning and confident, graceful and vulnerable, mature and in process. It was all there.

When I proposed the publication of a collection to Church Publishing, they were enthusiastic. We decided that the format most useful to the wider Church would be an anthology intended for devotional reading during Lent and Easter Week. Regrettably, this meant that some wonderful pieces had to be excluded—Christmas hymns, for example.

But within our stated purpose we decided to cast our net as widely as possible, so that there would be a characteristic variety of subjects and writing styles.

You'll want to have a *Hymnal 1982* at hand when reading this book, so that you can better connect the meditations with their subject hymns. Most readers will likely read this book from front to back—a meditation or hymn per day. But there's an index of topics and keywords at the back of the book in case you'd like to read these students' thoughts on a particular subject.

A few hymns served as inspiration for two different meditations. It's fascinating to compare what two authors found in the same hymn.

Perhaps a quarter of these meditations connect somehow with the subject of death. At first this relatively high percentage surprised me because seminary students generally are so life-filled and energetic. But these students taught me something: in the face of extreme duress, just as in times of great joy, people hold on tightly to their hymns. They sing them and allow themselves to be vulnerable. They allow the words and music to speak to their souls. Then they store all this in their memories to be recalled at some future time. Sometimes hymns can get done what can't get done any other way.

Seminary is about preparation, formation, and transformation; it's about living in Christian community. Seminary is a journey. In this book, students at the Seminary of the Southwest place before you something of their journey, some of the fruits of their labors. And they invite you to make this part of their journey part of your journey through Lent and Easter Week.

—RUSSELL SCHULZ-WIDMAR
retired in Berlin, Germany

The editor of this book and authors of these hymns and medi-tations intend that royalties from the sale of the book go to the Seminary of the Southwest.

Obtaining Permission to Reprint Hymns

If you would like to use any of the original hymns in this collection, please receive permission from the author. For current addresses, contact The Seminary of the Southwest, 501 East 32nd Street, Austin, TX 78705, 512-472-4133, or www.ssw.edu.

The Glory of These Forty Days

Meditation based on
"The glory of these forty days," *Hymnal 1982*: 143

The glory of these forty days
we celebrate with songs of praise;
for Christ through whom all things were made,
himself has fasted and has prayed.

We begin our Lenten days with ash on our foreheads and with the solemn reminder of our mortality: "Remember that you are dust, and to dust you shall return." Then, as Lent unfolds, we come to the singular Christian understanding: our frail bodies are meant for glory. Our bodies are the habitat of glory, of God's own radiant presence, revealed in Jesus. Our Friend and Companion in the way shares this embodied human life, and lives it from the inside out. He knows hunger, thirst, fatigue. He chooses fasting and prayer. He recognizes both the limitations of the body and its divine origin.

How can this be? We are surrounded by images that tell us the body is a commodity. Or that the body is nothing more than a means for gulping down food or booze or chemicals. We fail to see the body as the handiwork of God, as our own particular "text"—a little gospel of the good news of God's vital and eternal creating, as close as our breath, as intimate as the hand of a master artisan.

"The glory of these forty days" is precisely this: the reminder that when we fast and pray, we follow in the steps of Jesus. We act on the wild invitation of the Holy Spirit to enter the wilderness of Lent. We engage in fasting and prayer. We let go of the illusion of needing so much. We walk into the spare, open space of Lent and we begin to live in a clarity of body, mind, and spirit. We do so as a company, as the gathered community. We do so in the company of Jesus the Christ, "through whom all things are made." The Christ is with us, and we with him. Strength and grace will mark this journey. Each day of Lent potentially resounds with the Word speaking in and through our cells, our marrow, our muscles and sinew. Each day of Lent, limned with glory, invites us to cast aside illusions that we are self-sufficient or self-made. Each day of Lent calls us to venerate the image and likeness of God in the bodies of others, recognizing the sacred presence of Jesus in his various disguises.

This hymn reminds us of the gifts to be found in the way of Lent. We become a pilgrim people, walking together through the fasting and praying. We remember together the great stories of Scripture—Moses, Daniel, and Jesus each knowing their need and their weakness. We recall that the wilderness is the scriptural place of presence. The hymn, as it sings in us, brings us to adoration. We sing together of our God-given desire to love God, neighbor, and ourselves through these Lenten disciplines. As we fast, we recall those whose tables have no food, and those whose labor places food before us. We remember those bodies emaciated by famine, those eyes dulled by war, those minds battered by the fearful trek of the refugee. As we pray, we are knit together anew as the Body of Christ, Bread of Life. As our bodies and our spirits are gently refashioned and reclaimed by the Love who will not let us go, we discover anew that each wilderness is full of divine presence, full of possibility, full of that sacred Life that leads us to fast and pray with joy.

—MARY C. EARLE

Dame Julian's Vision

Refrain
    God holds the world, a hazelnut,
    and keeps us safe in hand.
    The love of God for each of us
    will every care withstand.

    Sometimes our lives are troubled,
    not tranquil or serene.
    But then dear Christ, our Mother,
    makes all our spirits clean.

    When Julian saw Christ's passion,
    she heard our savior say:
    God's everlasting mercy
    will never fade away!

    When pain and sorrow threaten
    as Julian did foretell,
    remember Christ's sweet promise
    that "all things will be well."

Words: Winifred Mitchell
© 2006
Possible Tune: *Balm in Gilead*

Journey to Christ

Meditation based on
"I bind unto myself today," *Hymnal 1982*: 370

I sat on my sister's bed, feeling as bleak as the winter day out-side. The gray, chilly winters in northwest Florida can fill one's marrow with dampness, and my bones were fairly dripping.

I sat alone. Gloomy. Bereft of comfort. The comfort of central heat: who could afford that anymore? The comfort of companionship: my sister had taken my son to a movie and the rest of our roommates were long scattered to the neighbor-hood malls.

My only company was the leftover rain dripping from the gutters and the smells emitted from my sister's old mattress—mildew and perspiration. Poor company for a lonely widow of twenty-four.

I sighed and thought about Larry, my husband, also gone. Gone to death. As usual, I had put on one of his T-shirts that morning—mostly all I wore on the weekends were a pair of softly faded jeans and Larry's T-shirts. I couldn't seem to part with them—it was too much like parting with him, so I kept them and wore them, notwithstanding the accusation of my four-year-old son some months prior. Pointing to my closet, he'd said firmly, "I *know* you have some dresses in there!" Well, he was right, but who was I going to dress up for?

I picked up one of the magazines my sister favored—
Good Housekeeping or *Redbook*—and flicked a particularly
skeletal looking model's bare thigh. "I know you have some fat
in there," I grumbled, hating her skinny, airbrushed self. Sigh.

"Deborah," I asked myself, "did anyone ever have a better fix on self-pity than you do right now?" Probably not, I
decided. Flipping to another page, I stared at an article's title
asking if a marriage could be saved. Huh. Well, mine can't. I
tossed the magazine on the floor beside the bed and flopped
back onto the pillows, tears streaming down my face.

Clink-clank. Ah, the mailman. Another big sigh and I was
off the bed, wrapping a wool shawl around my shoulders. At
least I could fetch the mail and distribute it to the roomies—
that would take up some of this dreary time on my hands.

Among the junk mail, circulars, and letters for the household I saw a legal-sized envelope with my name and address
typed on it. Great. Another Larry admirer telling me how sorry they are. Not as sorry as I am, I thought.

I plopped onto my sis's bed again and slid my thumb under
the envelope's seal and extracted a poorly typed, smudged
piece of onion skin.

What's this?

I began to read:

Christ be with me,
Christ within me,
Christ behind me,
Christ before me,
Christ beside me,
Christ to win me,
Christ to comfort
and restore me.

Christ beneath me,
Christ above me,
Christ in quiet,
Christ in danger,
Christ in hearts of
all that love me,
Christ in mouth of
friend and stranger.

Dearest Deborah,
*   I don't have any money as usual, but I wanted*
to send you a present. This was the only one I could
find that describes how I feel for us all, but especially
for you and Lance in our losing Larry.

It was signed with love from my cousin Carla. It was the best present I have ever received, and it helped to change my life.

—DEBORAH KEMPSON-THOMPSON

For another meditation on this hymn, see CALL TO MINISTRY, p. 19.

O Lord, to You Our Souls Are Raised

Paraphrase of Psalm 25

O Lord, to you our souls are raised;
show us your paths of love and faith.
Forgive us, Lord, our sins of youth;
teach us and lead us in your truth.

Our feet are plucked out of the net;
your mercy we shall not forget.
We trust in you all the day long;
remove our shame and make us strong.

To you, O friend, we turn our eyes;
have pity when you hear our cries;
When sorrows of our hearts increase,
deliver us and grant us peace.

Words: Lori Johnson
© 2003
Possible Tune: *The Eighth Tune*

Taste and See

Meditation based on "Taste and see,"
Lift Every Voice and Sing II: 154

Last Sunday I attended the jazz mass at St. James Episcopal Church with my family. Though I have always enjoyed worship there, I was moved in a different way with the addition of the musicians whose gifts were shared as a blessing to all of us present. I was especially struck by the postcommunion hymn, "Taste and see," as it seemed to create a nexus for me in my life: partaking of bread and wine at the Eucharist, community, and my role as a physician. It was this last identity to which my mind was drawn as I pondered the physicality of tasting and seeing. These are sensual verbs; these are verbs of bodily function, and they created for me a link to my Tuesdays spent in an exam room in a Killeen, Texas, family practice clinic, completing my commitments as a clinician. The activities of my Tuesday afternoons and evenings have become an integral part of each week—it is part of the ordered agenda of life for me, and I am thankful. I am thankful for the opportunity to participate in people's lives in such an intimate way. I connect with people as they entrust to me their stories of, among other things, difficulty swallowing, problems conceiving, and anxiety associated with a breast lump newly found.

Beyond the usual clinical analysis of history and physical

exam, beyond the education and reassurance provided to patients whose healing requires these medicinal arts, I am drawn to the intrigue of weaving these experiences—and explanations of their meaning—into the context of this hymn and, on a broader level, of worship in general.

The *body* and the *Body*

As a physician I am, among other things, a physiologist: I am a student of the function of the body. In this vein, function or physiology is an active verb, just as "taste" and "see" are. Liturgy, likewise, is active; it connotes work of the Body in its many parts.

Water

The human body is three-fourths water. It requires this much substrate for cellular functions to occur homeostatically, but, as important, it is water which, through its hydrostatic pressure, allows us to take form and even to stand erect. Without it, integrity of organs, including the skin, would cease to function as we know them to function. Similarly, the Body is hydroponic in nature: sacramentally, scripturally, and diaconally. It needs water to survive.

The story of the Body is rich in its wetness: primordial waters of creation, the water of the grave, Red Sea waters parting, water gushing from the rock in the wilderness, the immersion of Naaman in water, the water of Mary's womb, the Jordan River of crossing over and of baptism, the living water promised the woman at the well in Samaria, the healing pool of Bethsaida, the water gushing from the side of Christ on the cross, and the waters of Paradise. Our baptismal identity depends on the water: it is creative, it is womblike, it is mysterious, it is powerful, it is healing and life-giving, it is redemptive, it is passionate. This Body whose life is derived from water thus serves, cleanses, refreshes, and is relational.

Nourishment

In addition to water, the body requires caloric sustenance to energize the physiologic norms of the body. We find pleasure, comfort, even sensuality in the tastes and textures of food. We use it as a substrate for the functional nourishment of the body, but also for its communal properties.

The Body nourishes itself (and, indeed, all its parts) with the meal at the Table, but its claim is a seat at the greater family feast. The family, over food and wine, shares story, prayer, laughter, and sorrow anamnestically. The stories told have a common theme: God's provision of nourishment in all its forms. The stories are again rich in their nutrient power: the Passover meal; the feast told in Miriam's song; just enough manna and quail in the desert; a Promised Land of milk and honey; meal enough for Elijah, a widow, and her son; a wedding feast that saved the best wine for last; feeding 15,000 (when women and children are included); a feast for a prodigal son on his return; a last supper for and with friends. And perhaps most satisfying—a meal with a stranger at Emmaus, which in its glorious revelation relieved a hunger in two men who were famished by their recent loss of a dear friend and mentor.

In all these ways, through water, wine, and food, we taste and are able to see the goodness of God.

Hunger

For the physical body, hunger is an awareness, originating in nerve stimulation in the midbrain, which is perceived as a craving or even a noxious pain throughout the body. Its effects are systemic and, in extreme deprivation, it spares no part of the body the consequences of malnutrition. It is disruptive to the whole. The body in a hungered state simply wastes and withers, unable to maintain even basic bodily function.

Similarly, the Body that fails to find nourishment as depicted above will cease to experience its normative physiology. The hungry Body operates on a principle of scarcity incongruent with the real abundance found in God's creation. Parts of the Body take what they feel they need to function. Indeed, they hoard out of fear and do not share. And the Body still breaks down because its synergy is lost. And in the profoundly ironic crossing of symbols, the Body dies and desiccates without food and water fully shared. What started as dust returns to dust, and all seems lost.

New Life

But all is not lost. Through grace and God's unceasing offer of redemption comes new life in a resurrection of the Body. At a new crossroads between time as we know it and eternity as God makes it known through Jesus, the Body, restored to full health and wholeness, with all its parts, takes its seat at the Heavenly Feast in thanks and celebration for the one who invited us.

In anticipation of this ultimate experience, I find new perspective in my ministry as a physician. It stems from my baptized ministry, grounded in water, and I ponder how the stories shared with me in doctor-patient relationships, even focused on malfunctions of the body, somehow provide patient and physician with the opportunity to feed each other.

It is here, in the routine of life, with other people, that I am able to taste and see the goodness of God.

—STEVE THOMASON

And Grace Will Lead Me Home

Meditation based on
"Amazing grace! how sweet the sound," *Hymnal 1982*: 671

Do you have skeletons in your closet? I do—big time. I have been lost, I have been blind, I have been afraid. I have created and been surrounded by dangers, toils, and snares. I have felt wretched, and I have caused others to feel wretched too. But somehow, steadily, there has been amazing grace.

I think the first time I heard "Amazing grace" was in the early 1970s, when I was a war-protesting, bra-burning hippie-wanna-be listening to Judy Collins sing on the radio. A decade later, as I settled into the beauty and steadfastness of the Episcopal Church, "Amazing grace" was one of the standard hymns in my parish. Everyone knew the song, and we could all sing it lustily. And when we did, I always felt bathed in love—a love that recognized the mistakes I had made in my life and offered the grace which would, nonetheless, lead me home.

It was that grace that led me, almost ten years ago, to seek psychotherapy in order to deal with some of my skeletons. Part of it came from a childhood that included my parents separating and reconciling twice, divorcing once, remarrying, then divorcing again; periods of baseline subsistence (we called them the K-Mart Christmases), and the devastating illness of my father's alcoholism and ultimate death from that disease. As I began to work through my part in that drama, my therapist suggested I ask my mother for help in remembering the blocks of time that were blank to me. But when I asked Mom for help, she replied, through clenched teeth, "You cannot make me discuss the things I choose to forget."

That began a period of estrangement from my mother and my younger sister, who, likewise, could see no reason for revisiting the past. They lived in the Southwest, and my husband and I lived in faraway North Carolina, where I continued my therapy and began to experience the first stages of healing.

It was during this time that my sister had her first child. My mother was ecstatic about being a grandmother. My husband and I had decided not to have children. Once, unkindly, I told my mother that part of the reason was that I didn't want to risk putting a child through the same sadness I had felt growing up.

But yes, I certainly felt jealousy when my younger sister gifted my mother with that precious grandchild. My soul ached because I didn't know if we could ever bridge the gap that was between us.

Hours and hours of therapy later, my anger was spent. I wanted to begin making amends. I called my mother one evening. It was uncanny timing, because she told me that she had planned to call me that day too. She had been to the doctor, who diagnosed lung cancer, which had already spread to her liver and spine.

Have you ever had a crystal-clear moment when suddenly you knew the heart of a thing? When all of the words and events of time past condense into a little cartoon blip and are gone from the screen? On the telephone that night, during the first time I had spoken to my mother in over six months, I heard her voice shake with the news of the cancer, and without thought I blurted, "You're a good mama." I could hear her catch her breath. "And you're a good daughter," she replied. It turned out to be the best we could do.

Mom lived for four more months. I was able to spend six weeks of that time with her. The radiation and chemotherapy only made her more ill, so we moved her home, and my sister and I took turns administering, hour by hour, twenty-four hours a day, the morphine that numbed the hideous pain of the cancer that spread throughout her shrinking body.

I kept wishing for a Hollywood moment when Mom would say something that would make all those childhood years better. But she had so little strength. The only certain time her eyes would light up would be when we would carry my baby nephew into her room. Tyler was pudgy with "rubber-band wrists"—you know, the kind of baby fat that just bulges at all the joints? And he had huge, round, deep black-brown eyes that, even at ten-months-old, looked like they understood what was going on in that room.

I felt more jealousy. I wished Mom's eyes would light up the same way for me that they did for Tyler. But, mostly, we were all so exhausted that we did little more than make it through the minutes between the morphine.

I had to go back to North Carolina for some business. While I was there, Mom died. "Did she say anything?" I asked my sister. No, nothing. We had made the funeral arrangements months before. All I could think of was getting through it. I welcomed the glazed numbness.

Then I got a telephone call from a man who had worked with my mother for the past twenty years. She had been the manager, then part-owner, of a small petrochemical company, and he was one of the truck drivers. Emmet Parker was a barrel-chested African-American, by now in his sixties. We had always known that he was a preacher in his own church. He asked if he could sing at Mom's funeral.

It ticked me off. It made me crazy. I didn't even know if he could sing. And I certainly didn't want to mess with changing any of the details that were already in place. But I knew he and my mother had been good friends, not just coworkers. Oh, I was not gracious about it. I am certain my exasperation came through loud and clear. Still, I assented and told him to call the Lutheran pastor who was in charge. I just wanted it all to be over, so I could go back to North Carolina and sort out the confusion and despair that were in every breath I took. I wanted all sorts of things that, of course, were never going to be mine.

The family was ushered into the front of the church. Ten-month-old Tyler, my sister and her husband, and my husband and I were in the front row. It was as though I were inside a seashell, hearing the words amidst a dull and steady roar in my ears. My husband's arm encircled me. Then Tyler, that precious little bundle of cooing and soft baby smells, crawled along the pew into my lap. And from the balcony in the back of the church, a cappella, Emmet Parker began singing "Amazing grace."

> *Amazing grace! how sweet the sound,*
> *that saved a wretch like me!*
> *I once was lost but now am found,*
> *was blind but now I see.*

What did I see? I did not see all the answers I was yearning for. But I did see my mother's life as one of striving, of loving, of trying to make sense of the pain she never asked for. I saw her grandson, and I held him as he cuddled into my arms. I saw love, and I felt love.

Now it is years later. I know that my blindness was lifted that day and I saw with new eyes. I also know that there is so much more yet to see. Each time I sing "Amazing grace," I am reminded of that sweet, sweet truth.

'tis grace that brought me safe thus far,
and grace will lead me home.

(*Postscript 2011:* My sister died of colon cancer in 2005. Tyler, the apple of her eye, is now twenty-five, with an MBA and a successful start on a career in business. He has a serious girlfriend, but I haven't met her yet.)

The Lord has promised good to me,
his word my hope secures;
he will my shield and portion be
as long as life endures.

—Rhonda Smith McIntire

Three Persons Indwelling

Three persons indwelling, O God Trinity,
Love's dancing eternal, internal, and free.
Your love spilling over is fitting and right,
the gift of creation pours forth with delight.

Your perfect transcendence is nothing to fear;
your difference most different is what brings you near.
Both closer than matter and closer than time
you gift each uniquely with your love divine.

Unceasing diversity mirrors the One
swept into your Spirit through Jesus the Son.
Our difference no longer our suffering or pain,
our place in Christ's body most humbly we claim.

Invited to Love's dance, bestowed with Christ's kiss,
our first purpose only to receive the Gift.
The second flows from it: to rescue from strife
and restore creation to your triune life.

Words: Kathy Pfister
© 2009
Possible Tune: *St. Denio*

Reflections on the theology of Kathryn Tanner and noncompetitive transcendence: the idea that God's transcendence does not imply distance, but rather intimacy.

Call to Ministry

Meditation based on
"I bind unto myself today," *Hymnal 1982*: 370

It brought the "gift of tears," this song. Why should it be so? This crying without sadness or even the feeling of joy. Just crying. Why? What is the origin of these tears? From where do they flow?

They are born in a deep, deep place, an inner river of devotion and desire. They flow beyond the thoughts and arguments with which I try to fortify myself against commitment to the ordained ministry.

Who I am is truly beyond such arguments and feelings of fear or unworthiness. Like Jacob wrestling with the angel, my pilgrimage toward ordination has been a struggle. The grace of perseverance has brought me thus far. Just to commit to this time and place has meant saying a huge "yes" to God. *Thank you, most Holy Trinity*, for the gift of the deep places in our souls and in our lives where you stir and make yourself known. These are the places where you alone dwell.

So much is required to say yes, because so much has been relinquished. What do I have to give up? I have to surrender both fear and anxiety. It is the fear of power that lies dormant within me. For many years now, I have tried to hide this talent in the earth. I wonder: what would it feel like to not be afraid?

Thank you, most Holy Trinity, for the gift of courage to keep going and to move through fear.

I bind the name of the Trinity to myself. Because I participate in the life of God, merely speaking the Name makes me present to God's presence. Indeed, Lord God, you are closer than my next breath. Therefore I am no longer just named as I was at my physical birth, but my response to your call is a new birth. I am now named according to the life that has chosen me, the life I have surrendered to, the life of God. With my new birth comes the power to grow up in grace. "I am confident of this, that the one who began a good work among you will bring it to completion by the day of Jesus Christ" (Phil. 1:6). *Thank you, Lord God*, for the new birth and the gift of growing grace.

I am one with the life of Christ. It is no longer I, but Christ who lives in me . . . from his birth to his ascension where he sits on the right hand of God the Father. I am being forced to let die all that is not God. So my small, petty, self-centered, ungenerous, and ungrateful spirit must die as well as all of the thinking, thinking, thinking that can so easily lead down empty rabbit holes of self-pity or despair. The life of the Trinity is a life of abundance, not lack; faithfulness, not fear; radical love of other, not self-centeredness. It is a life of light, hope, and peace. My *habitus* has been to live in just the opposite way, living unto myself and failing to recall that I now live unto God. *Thank you, Lord God,* for the gift of the life of Jesus Christ.

I am one with all who worship and serve the living God in all time and in all places: the cherubim, the seraphim, the patriarchs and prophets, and all who confess the living God in Jesus Christ. Our participation in the Holy Trinity unites us. As well, I am one with all of the created cosmos. The loving fellowship of the Holy Spirit holds all in a net of infinite tenderness and strength. *Thank you, Lord God,* for the gift of all who have come before me and for the gift of creation. I am grateful for my heritage in faith.

This oneness in God means I am guided, protected, sustained, and taught of God by God. I have not yet apprehended . . . but I press on toward the goal for the prize of the upward call of God in Jesus Christ. *Thank you, Lord God,* for your immeasurable love that surrounds me on all sides.

The true life in the Three-in-One and One-in-Three takes up my life, setting it on fire and redeeming and transforming it into a life of love and healing in a web of interconnected relationships. Every relationship can show me God through the eyes of faith if I so allow. Who I know myself to be (my life and its purpose) is bound up in my name. My identity, which is uniquely my own, is also paradoxically the life of Jesus Christ. One day at the end of the ages, all will truly be Christ. And I, with the rest of the cosmos, will be completely one with the life of God. *Thank you, Lord God,* for restoring me and all of creation to yourself through the reconciling work of Jesus our Lord.

—Freda-Marie S. Brown

For another meditation on this hymn, see JOURNEY TO CHRIST, p. 5.

Each Day My Christ

Each day my Christ, my Christ my shield,
safe keep me in my standing.
Uphold me, son of David,
my strength in Christ unending.

Each night, my Christ security,
Preserve me in reclining.
Hold near, O son of Mary,
my peace in Christ unending.

Each light, each dark, my Christ shelter,
awake, asleep, encircling,
my triumph and treasure,
my life in Christ unending.

Words: Lance Peeler
© 2006
Possible Tune: *St. Columba*
In honor of Bryan Earle

Words adapted from a Celtic prayer beloved by Bryan:
My Christ! My Christ! My shield, my encircler,
each day, each night, each light, each dark;
be near me, uphold me, my treasure, my triumph,
in my lying, in my standing, in my watching, in my sleeping.

These Hands of Mine

These hands of mine I offer to your service,
to be your hands to those who need your care,
to feed, protect, embrace, lift up, and comfort
each part of your creation everywhere.

These arms of mine reach to your weary children;
use them to gather each and every soul.
Use them to hold each broken life as precious,
and give them strength to mend as you make whole.

This heart of mine is open to your wisdom;
through it I see and know that which is true;
a place where love flows out to feed creation,
and be the meeting place where I find you.

Words: Ann R. Johnson
© 2006
Possible Tune: *Hope of the World*

We Come, O Christ

We come, O Christ, as people seeking
some sign of blessing on our lives,
yet scarcely pause to hear you speaking
or wait until your time arrives:
help us let go, help us be still;
in patience may we learn your will.

To taste the cross within the chalice,
to hear the music born of grief,
to feel the hurt concealed by malice,
to sense in doubt unripe belief:
give us, O God, new hearts, new eyes;
wake us to love and make us wise.

Renewing Spirit, come breathe through us
with hope that heals, with faith that thrills;
burn off the sins still clinging to us,
transform our minds, convert our wills:
so may your gifts of grace increase
to send us forth in love and peace.

Unite our hearts and shape our living
to share the yoke that sets us free;
great Triune God, joined by self-giving,
the life of true community,
our many prayers at last make one:
"Your kingdom come, your will be done."

The Seminary Hymn

For two weeks in the spring of 1995 Carl Daw, Jr. and Alfred Fedak, along with four others engaged in hymn writing, were Visiting Fellows at the Seminary of the Southwest. At the conclusion of their stay, Daw and Fedak presented the seminary with a copy of a hymn: Daw's "We come, O Christ" set to Fedak's tune called *Rathervue*. Fedak had composed the music during his stay at the seminary. Most of Daw's text had been written earlier for another seminary, but eventually he added a new fourth stanza when it became clear that the hymn had become known to Southwest students as "the seminary hymn." It is now sung at all Seminary of the Southwest convocations and graduations.

A festival arrangement of this hymn for congregation and choir composed by Russell Schulz-Widmar is published by Selah Publishing Company at www.selahpub.com.

Rushing Waters, Jaunty Streams

Rushing waters, jaunty streams,
wiggling fishes, sunlit waves,
dizzy heights and silken skies,
sing to God your cry of praise!

Footprint canyons, ribbon creeks,
wind and watery voices speak.
All are but one sundry call
drawing to him one and all.

Make one voice in joyful song,
joining the angelic throng.
All God's creatures fired in love,
all below join heaven above.

Words: Benjamin Long
© 2008
Possible Tune: *The Call* or
Monkland

Morning Has Broken

Meditation based on
"Morning has broken," *Hymnal 1982*: 8

This morning in chapel we sang "Morning has broken." So many times I have sung this song! So often it sings itself silently in my heart! My spirit always leaps up with joy to meet it, this affirmation of all I intuitively know and believe about the gift and goodness of creation, all that is seen and all that is unseen, the Source from which it comes, the promise of a forever morning. The exultant "yes" of it!

I remember the first time I heard "Morning has broken." As I drove down the highway, I turned on the radio. Cat Stevens was singing it. Everything in me responded to it. A few weeks later, our family was camping in Utah. It was a fresh, new morning. As I prepared breakfast, my little boys waded in the creek a few feet away. My youngest son had asked me to put on the "Morning has broken" tape and, as it was playing, I watched with wonder the reflection of the sun on the rippling water and on those beautiful and precious little faces. *Morning has broken, like the first morning, blackbird has spoken like the first bird.* Somehow the bird singing that morning really *was* the first bird of creation, connecting us with the song that never ends.

The song became a special bond between my little son

and me. He had a speech problem, but he liked to sing with me. Singing was something neither of us could do well, but when we sang together, it never really mattered. *Praise for the singing*! Only here could I really allow myself to sing. How lovely the gift of being in the presence of one who loves you *just the way you are. Praise for them springing fresh from the Word*!

My son was seven when he died. Our priest said we could have anything we wanted for his funeral service. Two hymns immediately came to mind:

> *The strife is o'er: the battle done,*
> *the victory of life is won;*
> *the song of triumph has begun. Alleluia!*

And "Morning has broken."

One hymn so magnificent, the other so simple, but both with the same message: the song of triumph, the outburst of joy. Because he lives, we live. I sang both that morning. I sang with every fiber of my being, and meant each word with every beat of my heart. Amazing! In the midst of grief there is still a small space for joy.

Often, as I did the morning of that funeral service, I have to smile when we come to the last verse, *Mine is the sunlight! Mine is the morning born of the one light Eden saw play! Praise with elation, praise every morning, God's re-creation of the new day!* I smile because I see him, that frail little boy with the big, sparkling brown eyes, skipping in the sunlight, celebrating life, celebrating himself, claiming the promise of the new morning. Ours *is* the sunlight, ours *is* the morning, born of that one light, recreated again and again and again.

The first memorial service I was asked to do during my

CPE hospital residency was for a little baby I had baptized shortly after his birth. Just before he died, we sang "Morning has broken," his mother and father looking at me as we sang. Together, we affirmed the resurrection in the midst of grief.

Although I usually smile when I sing "Morning has broken," it is no shame that I also sometimes cry. The message of God's goodness, of his creativeness, of his resurrection, does not negate our grief. We are joined in it by the presence of the One who came to be with us, to be like us, the One who knows best what suffering is. Yet neither does the grief negate our joy, for joy is not the absence of suffering, but the presence of God. Truly, in that presence, morning *has* broken like the first morning, and truly, ours *is* the sunlight, ours *is* the morning! Praise for the singing, praise for the springing, praise for the sweetness, praise for the completeness.

—CAROL LUKE SPENCER

Carol Luke Spencer died unexpectedly of a heart attack on March 9, 2005. "Morning has broken" was sung at her funeral.

For another meditation on this hymn, see MY GRANDMOTHER'S GARDEN, p. 83.

Lord, Shine Your Light

Lord, shine your light upon this place,
and fill us with your wondrous grace.
Guide us in doing all we should
to spread the message as you would.

Help us respect the gifts of all,
and praise the blessing of our call.
Restore our sight that we might see
the strength of our diversity.

Let not our differences divide
but be forever by our side.
In your great love may we unite
our present, past, and future bright.

Words: Kiah Webster
© 2003
Possible Tune: *Old 100th* or *Truro*

The Christian Life

Meditation based on
"Eternal Spirit of the living Christ," *Hymnal 1982*: 698

Our prayers may be designated as praise, thanksgiving, petition, intercession, and confession. So too the hymns that we sing may be identified as songs of praise and thanksgiving, proclamations of the *kerygma* and creeds of the faith, stories that tell the history and doctrine of the Church, and prayers addressed to God.

This hymn is a prayer of request to the Holy Spirit. It begins with an address to the "eternal Spirit of the living Christ." Two words stand out in this address: eternal and living. Both of them provide us with images descriptive of God. *Eternal* identifies the timelessness, boundlessness, and otherness of God. *Living* conveys a sense of the presence and the dynamic activity of God in the here and now.

The first stanza of this prayer hymn describes in personal, individual, and particular terms our human situation. "I know not how to ask or what to say; I only know my need, as deep as life, . . . only you can teach me how to pray." Here two themes are expressed. The first is *need*. This word and idea is repeated in each of the prayer's three stanzas. The second is the *incarnational nature* of this prayer. That is, the need is described as "deep as life." Only the Spirit can teach me how to pray, and the petition asks, "Come, pray in me. . . ." In addition, the hymn concludes with the words, "My life in you, O Christ, your love in me." These thoughts and images give the sense of the indwelling of the Spirit and the initiative of that Spirit deep within the one who is praying. We are reminded of both St. Paul's emphasis on the body as the place of the dwelling of the Holy Spirit and of St. John's description of the Holy Spirit as the Comforter.

This prayer hymn could be called a contemporary psalm, as it is reminiscent of many biblical psalms. It is a very individual and personal plea to God the Holy Spirit to answer a need for the discernment of his purpose and will; it asks forgiveness for failure and deeds done amiss; and it requests vision and strength for service.

It is also didactic. It draws on scriptural ideas and images. In addition, it follows the pattern of Jesus' example in the Lord's Prayer: it moves from individual concerns of petition and confession to the recognition of the fulfillment of life in love and service both to God and to all humanity.

Having described the hymn as personal, individual, and particular, we might well question whether it belongs in a corporate service of worship. There are two reasons why an affirmative answer can be given to this question.

Although it is personal and individual, it is not self-centered. This is an important distinction. That is, it turns the one who prays it inward to the indwelling Holy Spirit in order that one may be drawn outward to love and to serve God and all humanity. The focus is on the action of the Holy Spirit and the movement is outward.

In addition, although the prayer identifies particular needs and petitions, they are those which can be described as universal to all who worship. Therefore, we can each pray this hymn from deep within us as we worship together.

This is a hymn of prayer that is particular yet universal, it is individual yet corporate. It turns one inward to discover God's purpose and will, to find vision and strength, in order that one may be drawn outward in love and service.

—Barbara K. Bloxsom

Heartsong

Meditation based on "Tell out, my soul,
the greatness of the Lord," *Hymnal 1982*: 437

My soul speaks
        to the glory
        you know.
You ask a blessing, an open-ended response,
        things my heart cannot imagine.
How is it that I your handmaid
        might be with child—
                it cannot be!

My soul knows the closeness of your promise.
Time and again I have heard your Word,
        today so pregnant with meaning.
"Can your heart bear me a home?
        Can I be of you, woman,
                body and soul?"

My soul wearies of the glory you speak.
    My spirit wells within me:
        "Only if it be your will!"
    I am poor, I am lowly,
        one of the anawim.
                Is remnant enough?

My soul rejoices in God, my Savior.
    "Be it done unto me according to your Word."
        Your servant I am, blessed of my Beloved.
    Misunderstanding and mystery I know.
        My joy and my silence
                each welcome this birth!

Speak, my soul, embody your great name.
    You are Lord, you are Savior.
        Become incarnate
through me and within me.
        True Emmanuel,
                "God with us."

Speak, my soul, embrace endless Love,
    in covenant relationship
        ending in beginning,
ever-renewed and everlasting.
        Here is my heart,
                my life-giving gift.

Speak, my soul, proclaim the mighty One,
  so known and so loved.
      How can I refuse?
  What words would express
      willingness without question,
            in following my heart?

Speak, my soul, announce your mighty deeds,
  remembering the stories and promises
      that make present the possible.
  How wonderful the knowing,
      You are my journey,
            and my journey's end!

Quiet, my soul, of my never-ending passion
  to search for the answers,
      to plumb the depths,
  of the whys and the wherefores,
      of this mystery
            called sonship.

Quiet, my soul, in the greatness of your might.
  You are alive and I know you live.
      Yet what does this mean?
  This simple obedience,
      is it once and for all?
            Or will you ask me again?

Quiet, my soul, in listening presence.
  A son is born, a son is given
      in fullness and light,
  bringing food and refreshment,
      redemption
                and life.

Quiet, my soul, in faithfulness and mercy.
  Let the children know your promises
      and their children yet unborn,
  the mystery of the Word made flesh,
      within the "YES!"
                of our heartsong.

AMY DONOHUE-ADAMS

This meditation may be used on the Feast of the Annunciation, March 25.

Known Only By Our God

Recall life lost amid God's grace,
our ancestors now gone
without a name, without a face,
and swept away without a trace.
On hallowed ground they trod,
known only by our God.

The remnants of their jubilee:
debris and rubble left.
All that we know, all that we see,
are those few fragments scattered free.
Erased from records kept,
in nothingness they slept.

We tell our story of the one
who blessed the bread and wine,
who wrote not word, who wrote not song,
who left no heir nor life lived long,
who vanished not in time.
Christ's victory sublime!

Our duty, right, and joy outburst;
our Savior's news receive,
that all who ache, that all who thirst
will dine and drink; the last are first!
But nothing do we leave,
save love and those who grieve.

O God, who calls us each by name,
knows hands and hearts of those
who have not grave, who have not fame.
God's Word pours out to all the same.
Oblivion deposed!
Our history composed!

Words: Caleb Crainer
© 2009
Possible Tune: *Repton*

Our Father

Paraphrase of the Lord's Prayer

Our Father, who in heaven abides,
how blessed is your Name,
your kingdom come, your will be done,
in earth and heaven the same.

Give us the food we need today
for body and for soul.
Forgive our sins as we forgive,
and help us to be whole.

Protect us from the tempter's snare
when we would go astray,
and keep our feet on your straight path,
our eyes on you, we pray.

Forever, and forever more,
our lips will sing your praise!
Yours is the kingdom, yours the power
and glory yours always!

Words: Kathy Glenn
© 1990
Possible Tune: *St. Flavian*

Bring Out the Festal Lights

Bring out the festal lights, make song;
lay out fine linen, white and pure.
O scattered, lost, and broken souls,
your place of honor is secure.

A feast of hope the Christ prepares.
Abounding joy and clapping hands
forever welcome longing hearts,
for God's own Son this meal commands.

A feast of joy the Church prepares.
Rejoice and drink with deep delight,
for Jesus Christ will prodigals
and castaways with saints unite.

Give thanks to God who gives us all.
Give thanks to Jesus, God's high priest.
Restored and whole, the people sing,
"Remember Christ and keep the feast."

Words: Lera Patrick Tyler
© 2008
Possible Tune: *Wareham*

An Inconceivable Incarnation

Meditation based on
"He is the Way," *Hymnal 1982*: 464

The language we use to try to understand who God is and our relationship with God not only helps form our theology, but becomes intuitive in our imaginations. Therefore the metaphors we use in trying to speak and imagine such things about God have power to shape our very being.

The language and metaphor of "He is the Way" is exceptional. The hymn feels uplifting and empowering. The words resonate with the singer's sense of being and the singer's intuitive sense of incarnation.

Imagine my surprise when I discovered this poem by W. H. Auden is in *The Hymnal 1982*. I've spent years in the Episcopal Church, but never knew this hymn. I would bet that I never saw it, not because it is difficult to sing, which it is, but because it stirs up images which are extraordinary, different, unusual. There are images that expand our idea of God, of Jesus; images that are troublesome, engaging, enlightening, thought provoking.

Jesus is the Way.

The way is Jesus, the guide is Jesus. I may not be totally clear as to which path, but when I follow Jesus, I will be on an adventure. Jesus' ministry was of reversal. What was socially acceptable was turned around. Jesus ate and drank with people who were so unlike the Pharisees as to be unacceptable.

Follow him . . .

When I follow him through the Land of Unlikeness, I see rare beasts. My presuppositions are set on end and no longer are tax collectors impure, but they are worthy to eat at Jesus' table. With God the impossible becomes possible. What I couldn't imagine before becomes the unique adventure. The people whose paths I cross perhaps I would not have chosen. This Christian adventure is the Land of Unlikeness, and it is full of rare beasts and unique adventures.

Jesus is the Truth.

The Truth has been spoken by God, and that Truth is re-presented in Jesus. This is so different from "Seek ye first the kingdom of God and its righteousness" and yet not so different. When I seek the Kingdom, what do I expect? Security, I suppose? But Jesus didn't stand for comfort and security, at least for those, like me, who have enough to eat and nice clothes to wear to the banquet. Once again, Jesus reverses the usual order.

Seek him . . .

Those of us who are comfortable and secure must seek Jesus in the Kingdom of Anxiety. When I seek Jesus in the Kingdom of Anxiety, then I will return to the source of all great joy. By avoiding the Kingdom of Anxiety, I will never return.

Jesus is the Life.

It is Jesus whose life is within me, as well as in the rare beasts I meet in the world. Jesus is in those whose paths I cross, if only I lift up my eyes and recognize them.

Love him . . .

Jesus is in the bread and wine that give me life. When I meet the gaze of those I encounter, I meet Jesus in the World of Flesh. That must be transforming for me, so that I may love as Jesus has taught us to love. When I truly love Jesus, and am wedded to him by sacrament and service, each occasion shall dance for joy. Each encounter will dance for joy. Each communion will dance for joy. Each birth will dance for joy. All the songs will dance for joy.

—Kathy Monson Lutes

For another meditation on this hymn, see HE IS THE WAY, p. 76.

I Surrender All

Meditation based on
"I surrender all," *Lift Every Voice and Sing II*: 133

Almighty and eternal God, so draw our hearts to you, so guide our minds, so fill our imaginations, so control our wills, that we may be wholly yours, utterly dedicated to you; and then use us, we pray you, as you will, and always to your glory and the welfare of your people; through our Lord and Savior Jesus Christ. Amen.

A Prayer of Self-Dedication
The Book of Common Prayer, 832

Surrender is an odd word. In common usage, there is no sense of the word that has positive connotations. We surrender our legal rights in contractual disputes. We surrender ourselves to loss and grief. And although surrendering ourselves to our enemies in war may in fact save lives—even our own—deep down we know that what we have surrendered is our dignity, our pride. To surrender is to diminish ourselves; to become less than what we were.

Yet for Christians, it is in the essence of this word that we find redemption and renewal. It should tell us something about the God we serve that even language itself becomes redeemed through the cross of Christ. To the believer, words like "less," "weak," "die," and "surrender"—words that normally denote failure—convey instead the very life of God. But if language itself undergoes conversion, it is only because there is real, ontological change that occurs when God acts.

In Van DeVenter's hymn we begin with propositional statements rather than with words of devotion. "All to him . . . I will ever love and trust him . . . in His presence . . . humbly at his feet." Indeed, in the first part of the hymn we make our confession. We express to ourselves, to others, to anyone who will listen, that it is Jesus to whom we lay down our lives, Jesus who we will ever love and trust, Jesus in whose presence we will dwell, and Jesus at whose feet we bow. Our confession displays our intention.

But this *lex orandi*, this prayerfully intentional aspect of our commitment, is not enough. We cannot dwell in a faith that remains purely objective, dedicated only to propositions and statements of faith. Such a faith eventually grows cold and stale. Thankfully, it is the nature of the objective faith—the Scripture and the Creeds—that it draws us deeper into the life of God. Though we may contemplate Christ for years, studying him and learning about him, *lex orandi* eventually inspires *lex credendi*, and we find ourselves, like the hymn writer, pleading: "Take me Jesus, take me now."

At this point in our spiritual walk we begin to understand that we are, indeed, participants in the very life of God, and this knowledge highlights our need for utter devotion and the complete giving over of ourselves to the divine. Compared to this new life in Christ, worldly pleasures—what Jesus called the lust of the flesh, the lust of the eyes, and the pride of life—may seem more trivial than sinful. The fact that our worldly desires may do harm to our quest for Christ-likeness pales in comparison to the fact that they offer no help. The pursuit of obedience gives way to deep love of the divine. Following Christ, imitating Christ out of love for Christ, becomes the focal point of life.

With "worldly pleasures all forsaken," we empty ourselves and open ourselves up to new and profound depths of God's life. We are filled with the Holy Spirit, the very same Spirit that dwells in God's tri-union expression, that we may know divine power. As Paul tells us:

> Now we have received, not the spirit of the world, but the spirit which is of God; that we might know the things that are freely given to us of God. Which things also we speak, not in the words which man's wisdom teacheth, but which the Holy Ghost teacheth; comparing spiritual things with spiritual. (1 Cor. 2:12–13, KJV)

By the indwelling of the Spirit of Christ we are made wholly Christ's, utterly dedicated to Christ, and shaped in his image, not only for our own blessing, but for the blessing of others. The love and power that we are filled with are not for our own sanctification, but for the sanctification of the world. The double cry to be filled with the divine power of God is born in the understanding that in and through our surrender we are changed; transformed into agents of God's love. As Paul continues: "For who hath known the mind of the Lord, that he may instruct him? But we have the mind of Christ" (1 Cor. 2:16, KJV).

The surrendering of ourselves does not mean the dissolution of our persona or the annihilation of ourselves into nothing. It is, rather, nothing less than incarnation. The abandoning of ourselves to God does not destroy the self, but recreates it. It is and is not the old person. Just as Jesus was as much divine as he was human, without division or separation, in perfect and harmonious union, so we find ourselves perfectly joined by the Spirit to the Spirit.

And so we grow, from surrender to surrender, from conversion to conversion, ever spiraling upward toward God, abandoning more and more at each step along the way, that we might be filled with even greater power, covered with even greater blessings. Thus we find ourselves in the end full of the Spirit, wishing there were yet more that could be surrendered, and crying to God with our whole heart:

I surrender all,
I surrender all;
all to thee my blessed Savior,
I surrender all.

—KEVIN DELLARIA

All Things Bright and Beautiful

Meditation based on
"All things bright and beautiful," *Hymnal 1982*: 405

To a biology teacher and an evolutionist, the line "All things bright and beautiful, all creatures great and small, all things wise and wonderful, the Lord God make them all" sounds ludicrous at worst or naïve at best. Yet that line and the hymn, written by Cecil Frances Alexander, remain central to my worldview. We sang "All things bright and beautiful" in every chapel service at Canterbury, the Episcopal private school where I spent my early childhood. The hymn was one of the few things I looked forward to in chapel, and I still remember it by its old hymn number, 311.

This hymn speaks of the beauty of creation and therefore the beauty of its creator. It instilled in me a wonder at the natural world that would contribute to my desire to study biology and evolution. The hymn also deepened my faith so much that no biological theory of the existence of life could shake it. So I live in a natural world that I can analyze down to the cell, the molecule, even the atom, and yet as I look deeper into the natural workings of cellular biology, genetics, evolution, DNA, and biochemistry, all I still see is the hand of God and the beauty of his creation. The beauty of our God-created world still continues to teach and mold me to this day.

Each little flower that opens . . .

Can you imagine the hand of God? The very hand that formed the heavens and the earth? "My hand laid the foundation of the earth, and my right hand spread out the heavens; when I summon them, they stand at attention" (Isa. 48:13).

There is a nebula that has been found twenty-six billion light-years from earth. It takes light only nine minutes to reach the earth from the sun, but the light from this nebula takes twenty-six billion years to reach us. When you look at the closest star, Alpha Centari, you are seeing light that left the star four and a half years ago.

Yet God's hand formed and spread out these marvelous celestial bodies. The hand of God is mighty, powerful, and huge, yet it is gentle, thoughtful, loving. The hand that stretches out the heavens is the same hand that opens the fragile petals of a flower and makes the tiny wing of a bird. When we are in our most insecure or helpless times, it is good to remember the gentleness of the hand of God. "For I, the LORD your God, hold your right hand; it is I who say to you, 'Do not fear, I will help you'" (Isa. 41:13).

The purple-headed mountain . . .

Growing up in Florida, I did not see many mountains. I come from a land better known for its rivers, waterways, and beautiful sunsets and sunrises. A river is an amazing thing to watch. On a trip in the Everglades, I sat and watched the Harney River rush by my kayak as I rested on the shore. I had been working my way upriver against its natural flow on top of an outgoing tide, and I was tired of fighting the constant, unrelenting flow.

A river is a lot like God, always moving with purpose and energy. A river provides resources and water to all who are around: plants, animals, and humans. Rivers provide beauty, joy, enjoyment, and peace. God provides all the same and more. That day the river was telling me in its gentle and relentless way that I should move with her, not against her. Isn't that like God? When we go against God's flow and movement, God gently but persistently and unrelentingly beckons us to change our course. The river is relentless, and so is our God!

The cold wind in the winter . . .

I love a good tomato, not the ones you find in the supermarket. I think they should call those tomatoes what they are: red tasteless orbs. The best tomatoes are the ones you grow in your backyard. I planted a garden in my backyard two years ago. The garden taught me a lot about God. My three-year-old son "helped" me in the garden. It only took three times longer with his help, but the experience and time spent with Zach was worth a hundred times the setbacks. Zach "helped" me throughout the experience, from preparing the soil, to planting the seeds, to the final harvest. He pulled off the flowers to give to his mom. Great for Mom, but not helpful if you want fruit to grow. Zach "trimmed" branches, stepped on plants, and pulled unripe fruit. Yet with all of Zach's help, we had a great harvest and a great time. We ended up with more tomatoes than we could eat, along with carrots, cucumbers, peppers, and radishes. The tomatoes were the best tomatoes I've ever eaten, not because I grew them in the backyard, but because *we* grew them in the backyard. The endeavor was more relational, that of father and son, than of labor and produce. One of my favorite pictures is of Zach and me holding up the harvest in front of the garden.

I wonder if all of our endeavors to "help" God straighten out this world are like Zach helping me in the garden. Although we mess up, God does not mind, because he loves being with his children. God will provide the harvest, "the ripe fruits in the garden." We should focus on the relationship, not the product. God cares more about who we are than what we do or produce.

He gave us eyes to see them . . .

The hymn "All things bright and beautiful" is not my favorite hymn, but it certainly has had an impact on my life. It forces me to refocus my eyes to see as a child again, to see the wonders of creation, and to stop analyzing them all of the time. This hymn reminds me to seek the joy and beauty in creation. This hymn reminds me to share that beauty and joy with others, and to remember how "great is God Almighty," who was, and is, and ever will be. "All things bright and beautiful" forces one to turn off the eyes of judgment and focus once again on the beauty and brilliance of creation, and the beauty and brilliance of the creator.

—James Hedman

My Shepherd Will Supply My Need

Meditation based on
"My Shepherd will supply my need," *Hymnal 1982*: 664

I imagine myself to be the sheep: rather fetid as most farm animals will be. Not real clever. I tend to follow the throng. My fleece, tangled and matted, is nevertheless of rich quality. A fine garment it would make.

Useful but needy, this poor sheep needs a shepherd. A shepherd to lead me to fresh pasture and to find good water. A shepherd who will search me out when I run and hide from the flock. A shepherd with sturdy staff who shields me from predators.

A stormy night in the dark, alone, cold and frightened, I hear his whistle and I know I am safe. He scoops me up in his strong arms, slings me over his broad shoulders, carries me home. Home to my flock. His flock. He is always near.

I am me again. Sheeplike still in many ways. At times stubborn. At times foolish. I've been known to bite the hand that feeds me or kick someone who just wants to love me. But you, O God, shepherdlike in your love, are always near. One word from you calms my fears, if I listen. If I listen, I will hear your voice.

Call me back, O God, back to your flock, to share my gift, the beautiful wool which adorns me. Without your flock, without you, I am without purpose. Without your flock, without you, my gift remains unoffered. Without your flock, without you, my work is without meaning.

Call me back, O God, O my Divine Shepherd. The wool I give is my life in praise to you, Most Holy One. I find rest in you. I will listen. I will love. Home at last.

—Matthew R. Rowe

If I Give Up My Voice Today

If I give up my voice today
will you breathe out your Word?
I pray you to explain away
your quietness, O Lord.

What certainty I had in you
was delicate and spare;
the more I held what seemed so true
the less I found was there.

So can our hearts true sureness hold
while fragile Earth's our home?
Are you within this troubled world
or are we all alone?

Then let me find within the space
marked off by quiet prayer,
a glimmer of your countenance
to transport and to share.

A whisper in a silent place
with resonance outside;
"My Word is written in the face
of Jesus crucified."

Words: Rich Frontjes
© 2003
Possible Tune: *St. Flavian*

An Evening Prayer

The dusk now mingles with the dying day:
Come, stay with us, Lord Jesus Christ, we pray;
as spirits dim at setting of the sun,
burn bright within our hearts, O Holy One.

And when your light is hid from human eyes
by worldly glare, like stars in city skies,
burn brighter, Morning Star, and give us sight
to see you, far or near, by day or night.

Keep watch with those who work, or watch, or weep;
give peace to troubled minds, and grant us sleep,
that sleeping, we may rest within your grace,
and rested, we may rise to run the race.

And as we run, though we may err and stray,
Lord Christ, be our companion on the way:
run to us, catch us up in your embrace,
and lead us to your heavenly dwelling place.

Words: Eric Mellenbruch
© 1999
Possible Tune: *Sursum Corda* or
Song 4

Laetare

Meditation based on
"Joyful, joyful, we adore thee," *Hymnal 1982*: 376

From my teenage years "Joyful, joyful we adore thee" has been one of my favorite hymns. It certainly contrasted with the overabundance of exceedingly pietistic "life is crummy but will get better over yonder," redemption/fall ("covered with the blood of Jesus") hymns that I had sung as a child. Religion that asked me to bewail my plight and flee from sinful human existence was not so appealing to this teenager. "Joyful, joyful" instead presented me with a creation-centered spirituality. It's a celebration of life. It's a call to live and love joyfully.

After many years of theological study and intellectual pursuits, I still find the theme of this hymn to be outside the mainstream of theological thought. The great theologian Krister Stendahl points out how this shift from creation-centered spirituality toward personal salvation began:

> With Augustine, Western Christianity with its stress on introspective achievements started. . . . Man turned in on himself, infatuated and absorbed by the question not of when God will send deliverance in the history of salvation, but how God is working in the innermost individual soul. . . . The introspective

conscience is a Western development and a Western plague. . . . It reached its theological climax and explosion in the Reformation, and its secular climax and explosion in Sigmund Freud. (*Paul Among Jews and Gentiles* [1978], 16).

Matthew Fox is among a very few theologians who dare to articulate the creation-centered theology of this hymn. For Fox, wisdom is defined by living life to its fullest. To live is not to survive, but a passionate call to joy:

Living implies beauty, freedom of choice, giving birth, discipline, and celebration. . . . Joy beyond measure is part of everyone's potential experience. It is part of recovering an erotic God who plays, takes pleasure, births, celebrates, and feels passion. Eros and hope are part of the blessings of existence. (*Original Blessing*, 19)

This creation tradition, though falling out of favor with many theologians, has been kept alive by artists, scientists, and poets. And a few in the field of religion have recognized its significance. Gerhard von Rad states, "Creation not only exists, it also discharges truth. . . . Wisdom requires a surrender, verging on the mystical, of a person to the glory of existence" (*Original Blessing*, 35). In Anglicanism, William Temple has been the leading advocate of such a spirituality. Temple has pointed out that Christianity is the most materialistic of all religions. That is, Christianity concerns itself with matter, the stuff of human existence, placing a high value on that which is created by our Creator. Creation-centered spirituality views salvation as blessing rather than as deliverance.

The theme of this hymn is the very biblical notion that joy flourishes in the presence of God. In stanza one, God is the Sun, the author of light. As God of glory, She is also Lord of love. Thus in God's presence hearts unfold and bloom like flowers. The brightness of the Sun melts the clouds of sin and sadness and drives dark doubt away. God imparts gladness, which is immortal. Thus we ask that we would be filled with such light, the light of day. In this relationship we can only rejoice and adore the Giver of such beauty and love.

In stanza two, our focus shifts from God as Sun to God's creation. For in this good creation we are called to rejoice also. The creation reflects God's goodness ("earth and heaven reflect thy rays"). God remains the constant center of praise while creation literally surrounds the Creator with joy. Stars, angels, fields, forests, vales, mountains, meadows, seas, birds, and fountains all praise God by being what it is they are created to be. Thus, we are called to be what we are created to be, rejoicing in our Creator.

In stanza three, we remain in this creation, but a new twist is added. First, God's primary qualities of giving, forgiving, and blessing are celebrated. God is portrayed as the never-ending, never-depleted Source of the joy of living and happy rest. Creator and created are a family (God our father, Christ our brother), for all who live in love belong to God. And there's more. There is a sense in which we have not fully arrived or completely comprehended this blessedness we are given. Thus we ask God to teach us how to love each other, that we might truly be lifted to this ultimate joy, which is divine.

—BILL MILLER

Struggling with the Voice

Meditation based on
"Profetiza," by Rose Martha Zarate, *El Himnario*: 265

Refrain:
Prophesy, my people,
prophesy one more time,
that your voice may be the echo
of all people in oppression.

Prophesy, Hispanic people,
prophesy one more time,
announcing to the poor
a new society.

Prophet, I consecrate you.
Let there be no doubt or fear
as you journey through history;
be faithful to your mission.

Announce to his people
that God will renew
his covenant of justice;
his love will flourish.

Denounce all those
who cause oppression,
so that they will repent
and return to their Lord.

Let this be your hope,
let this be your mission:
to be the builder of the kingdom,
the society of love.

My hour of grace is at hand.
Sacrament of God,
be a sign of our solidarity;
be the Light of the New Sun (Creation).

—Translated from the Spanish
by Albert R. Rodriguez

My meditation takes the form of a dialogue with that mysterious Voice that seems to dominate the center stage of "Profetiza." Is this exhorter male or female? No, it is a neutral voice. But there is no question that it is a commanding voice, a righteous voice, a timeless voice that has the full sweep of history at its command. The Voice sounds like it has raised up prophets before.

"Are you the voice of the Holy Spirit?" I ask. "Are you that voice that gave impetus and courage to the ancient prophets?"

The Voice doesn't answer.

My meditation in the wee hours of the morning takes a dramatic turn, for I find myself being enveloped in the presence of the Voice. The feeling is one of awe, of a profound and bottomless something. I rarely have those profound feelings of reaching into my finite and innermost center where the

Infinite resides. No longer am I just meditating on the message of the hymn and hermeneutically analyzing its content. It is a raptured feeling of union with the sacred. I feel that lump in my throat and involuntarily getting misty-eyed, which is a good sign that the Voice and I have interacted before.

Identify yourself, Voice! For I have heard you before! Funny that you have not made yourself present to me before in Rose's "Profetiza."

How many times have I sung her words with gusto at San Francisco de Asis? But I have felt nothing of what I am feeling now.

Why am I particularly sensitive to the prophetic message at this point? It may be that my mind is currently on the theme of the liberation of the oppressed. As I reread the hymn, I can better understand why Rose had to put your message to print: she really had no choice. Like Rose, deep in the recesses of my mind and heart, I have also heard your incessant and unmistaken clamor of urgency. Aren't you that tortuous and nagging Voice that has brought me kicking and screaming to seminary? I am beginning to see who you are. I am beginning to recognize your footprints.

Prophesy, you say. First I thought you were talking to Everyman, the Prophet. But you are really talking to me, aren't you? Just like you kept trying to jolt me out of my lethargy and I kept putting you off. "Prophet, I consecrate you," you said. Hah! You do remember what I told you when I first heard your Voice? Something about not being worthy, or not knowing what right words to say, or that I was too earthy to be in your priestly ranks. And you responded, "Let there be no doubt or fear as you begin your journey. Be faithful to your mission." I had not equated your response with the words in "Profetiza," but you are used to working with reluctant and unprepared prophets, aren't you?

Prophesy, Hispanic people, announce that a new society is at hand. Rose interpreted you to mean the freeing of the marginalized and oppressed people, but I also see your prophetic words to announce to our tradition-bound Church that a new society is at hand. Isn't it ironic, Voice, that among other things you are using the marginalized people in Rose's hymn to help free up the monolingual, the monocultural, the monodimensional Church? Wake up, sons and daughters of Canterbury! Just as I was brought kicking and screaming into your fold, our Church has to be brought kicking and screaming to your people who lie beyond the suburban citadels that so much influence how we react to you.

Be the builder of the kingdom, you command. It almost seems that we've been trying to do this since we last heard your earthly Voice a couple millennia ago. *Let this be your hope,* you keep urging us. I can accept that, for hope is what keeps me going. Like Martin, I have a hope and a dream that some day Episcopal churches will be a reflection of our new society.

See what you've done, Voice, you and Rose. You keep insisting on this urgency business. You so resoundingly announce that the hour of grace is at hand, but I can feel my skepticism creeping in again. I guess that the feeling of the Infinite has left for now, and I'm beginning to see just the words of the hymn again. The hearing and the seeing with my inner eye are gone now. A pity that these occasional signs of grace, these rare moments of union, are difficult to evoke! It takes somebody like the Voice and instruments like Rose and "Profetiza" to sweep us up into a euphoric interlude, which is indeed a Sacrament of God.

May we be occasional true lights of the New Sun.

—ALBERT R. RODRIGUEZ

The Trinity

Our God exists in realms unknown,
beyond the bounds of history.
In persons Three, in nature One,
complete, divine community.

One loves; another love receives;
the third, the love, their unity.
This feast of love, we know not how,
brings forth creation's mystery.

Unchanging and yet ever new
the life they share, this Holy Three,
who still as One together dwell,
eternal love, the Trinity.

Words: Roxanne Ruggles
© 2010
Possible Tune: *Rockingham*

Awake, Awake to Love and Work

Meditation based on
"Awake, awake to love and work," *Hymnal 1982*: 9

In spite of the dry summer, the oaks are laden with acorns and the pecans are abundant. The squirrels are happy. For weeks now they have been collecting these fruits of the trees, carrying some to their nests, eating others on the spot, digging yet others into the ground to be retrieved later.

Invariably, some of these buried nuts will be forgotten. I will find them come spring, emerging from the dark warming earth as twiggy shoots. Left undisturbed and given the typical amounts of Texas rain and sun, they will slowly, gradually, many human lifetimes from now, be superb, multibranched, thick-leafed, and venerable creatures, worthy to be named *tree*.

It is a peculiar thought, that holiness is contained in the ordinary. Our wont is to connect holiness with the extraordinary: with bushes that burn for no apparent reason, with pillars of fire, incomprehensible victories over superior foes, choirs of angels and a shining star. And I suspect that these are indeed glimpses of holiness and highness.

But I also suspect that they are only fleeting and tantalizing suggestions of the true holiness that comes born out of the ordinary: Jesus called the Christ.

The extraordinariness of Jesus resides in his ordinariness. He was one of us. Yet through him flowed the holiness of God, manifested in his *liturgia* of love as he healed people, taught them, fed them, forgave them, died for them, and gave them new life through his resurrection. Holiness did not enclose Jesus and separate him from the world; rather, it was born out of him and connected him to it.

Holiness still flows outward, connecting God's creation to him. It flows out in the dawning of new days, the blessings of new births, the renewal of baptisms, in the new life of resurrections. Like all of these things, it flows from darkness to light, from not being to becoming. It resides in the common things of the earth. It resides in us. It yearns—demands—to be born.

And how we fight that birth! For we know that it must cause us pain, and pain, our world tells us, can and should be avoided. Anesthetize it, walk away from it, cover it up, deny it. Pain is a pain.

What happens, though, if we refuse to give birth to the holiness that waits within us? Very simply, we die. Birth will not be denied.

Just as the buried acorn that does not sprout rots in the ground and dies, our holiness can be smothered and crushed. The difference is that God refuses to let that holiness rot away; for, after all, holiness is a thing of God, not of the world. In resurrection God overcomes our reluctance to give birth and coaxes forth that holiness and, as he always does, holds us close in our pain.

But birth is never an end, only a beginning. And the great gift of God's holiness that bursts forth demands something: to love, to work, to give, to spend ourselves, to serve God gloriously.

In the late thirteenth century Meister Eckhart wrote:

Human beings ought to communicate and share all
the gifts they have received from God. If a person
has something that she does not share with others,
that person is not good. A person who does not
bestow on others spiritual things and the joy that is
in them has in fact never been spiritual. People are
not to receive and keep gifts for themselves alone, but
should share themselves and pour forth everything
they possess whether in their bodies or their souls as
much as possible.

To such a thought I can only conclude, "Awake, awake
to love and work."

—Cecilia Smith

Like Drops of Dew

Like drops of dew in morning mist arising,
our souls ascend, transformed before the Son.
As flame meets flame to brilliant blaze aspiring,
so hearts join hearts to burn with love as one.
Thus prayers like breath to breeze are ever swelling,
then breeze to wind and wind to mighty gale,
till all the saints in Blessed Spirit dwelling,
unbend the knees; arise; as one in Christ prevail.

One body we though blessed with many visions;
one cup, one bread, one life within us reigns.
One body fit with multiple divisions,
equipped to serve the world in Jesus' Name.
O may we hand in hand go forth together;
a mighty force to free, to heal, to love;
and glorify our merciful Creator,
till earth shall be as one with heaven above.

Words: Stephanie Swinnea
© 2003
Possible Tune: *The Derry Air*

In Winter's Grip

In winter's grip, the earth lies cold,
the seeds below unseen.
Spring warms the tender shoots to life;
the barren ground grows green.

Sarah and Abraham grew old
without the promised heir.
How Sarah laughed to bear her child!
Joy born out of despair.

Once Jesus hung upon the cross,
forsaken and alone.
The darkness sealed his tomb until
love rolled away the stone.

The widow cries, "O Lord, how long?"
The bridegroom sings, "Amen!"
God's listening breath sustains them both.
We die. We rise again.

There is no death God cannot raise,
no loss he cannot fill.
Give hope, O Lord, to those who wait
the flowering of your will.

Words: Lisa Stolley Hines
© 2006
Possible Tune: *Georgetown*

Celestial Hymns

Celestial hymns are sung to the Spirit.
So grateful our hearts at moments like this.
We smell homemade bread, the foretaste of heaven,
enchanted by grace and smitten with bliss.

Celestial dreams, ethereal beauty
transport our mind's eye above and beyond.
Like snapshots of God at home with the angels,
each glimpse is as if a spiritual wand.

Celestial peace through paintings of glory.
What now comes in clouds will one day be clear.
May hope calm our core when we get impatient,
and love be a sign of heaven right here.

Words: Rusty Edwards
© 2011
Possible Tune: *Celeste*,
by Carlton R. Young
Dedicated to Celeste Jouanet
Used by permission of Selah
Publishing Corporation,
www.selahpub.com.

Now

Meditation based on
"Now the silence," *Hymnal 1982*: 333

Now the silence . . . Now the peace . . .

For so long I have been afraid and have run from silence. Afraid of the loneliness I was sure would meet me there; afraid of the secret and forbidden thoughts; afraid most of all that there I might finally have to face the most frightening thing of all: myself. So unsure, so guilty, so afraid. Unable to live today, consumed by the guilt and remorse about the past; uncertain and afraid about the future. Seeking serenity and peace in business, distractions, fantasies. Hoping to find you somehow in constant striving, searching, doing. Looking for you in the childish fantasies of my past, in the hopes and dreams that somehow in the future something or someone will relieve me of the responsibility of facing life the way it is today. In the past I do not find you, the future is but an illusion. In the silence, in the living of this moment now, in the letting go of the past and the future, you meet me. Now, in this moment, you bring me peace. Now, in the silence, I am able to hear.

Now the empty hands uplifted . . .

Hands. So busy, searching, grabbing, striving. Things accumulated, hoarded, longed for. Hoping something can be seized, possessed that will assure me I am valuable, lovable, okay. Empty hands. Fingers that no longer serve to hold tightly, grab, possess. Letting go, reaching up. Hands in prayer, supplication. Hands met, held, embraced.

Now the hearing . . .

Things heard, as if for the first time. Weakness, loneliness, despair overcome by gentle power. Hope renewed, fear rejected. Wine, bread. Words said, promises remembered. How? Why? For me? Mystery I cannot explain, mystery I must accept.

Now the body, Now the blood . . .

Wine become blood, bread become Body. Body broken for me, blood poured for me. Undeserved, unearned. Freely given, pure gift. Holy gift from holy love. Love incarnate, love mysterious. Love that awes me, love I celebrate. Love that draws me, love that frees me.

Now the Spirit's visitation . . .

Holy Trinity. Awesome power, awesome love. Brokenness healed, wholeness restored. Love reaching out to me, love embracing me. Gratitude and awe. Blessed, loved, chosen. Joy complete, silent peace.

Now . . . Now . . . Now . . .

—JOHN B. MUSGRAVE

Symphony of All Creation

Symphony of all creation;
chorus of unbounded love,
joined by angels ever singing
to the wondrous God above.
We in union join the chorus;
glorious evermore we cry.
God, creator, source of goodness,
yours the majesty on high.

Instruments of God resounding;
glorious in their resonance.
All creation joins in chorus,
worshipping in holy dance.
Tune our hearts to play in rhythm,
praising, worshipping as one.
May we all, our souls uplifted,
celebrate God's gift, his Son.

Words: Jean McGraw
© 2009
Possible Tune: *Hymn to Joy*

He Is the Way

A Meditation on
W. H. Auden's "He is the Way," *Hymnal 1982*: 464

Throughout the poetry of W. H. Auden (1907–1973), to speak of night is to imply day; aloneness, togetherness; sorrow, joy; satisfaction, hunger. As in the work of his nineteenth-century mentor, John Keats, beneath simple implication works the highly Romantic longing for wholeness that remains as yet unattained. For Auden, what is addressed only in part may imply, in any given instance, what he understands to be his life and his world.

There is the sense in Auden's work that opposition and its consequential wholeness reaches right into the heart of his expressions of faith—for example, in his marvelous hymn in the *Hymnal 1982*, "He is the Way." This is a fragment from a long poem written by Auden in England as World War II was ending, seven years after Auden had become an American citizen.

Early on in his literary career, Auden applied himself to Marxism, following many young, committed intellectuals of his day. Through the social empathy the poet saw nurtured by this ideology, he found himself on a journey that, he felt, had to be reclaimed as spiritual. Essentially, what had begun in rage then grew into irony and cynicism. Ultimately his conscious detachment that is evident in his work at that time grew into a greater commitment to exploring the nature of paradox itself. By the end of the 1930s, in the face of the horrors about him, the pursuit of paradox became a commitment to personal and religious surrender and embrace.

Auden's consummate vision details humanity, not in its empty post-Victorian ideals, but rather in the postmodern existentialism of human suffering in the fact of the collapse of idealism. He wrote in "Musée des Beaux Arts":

> *About suffering they were never wrong,*
> *the Old Masters: how well they understood*
> *its human position; how it takes place*
> *while someone else is eating or opening a window*
>   *or just walking dully along.*

As brilliant as Auden's poems are, they generally do not contain ideas that require Christian faith. The process of conversion is benchmarked from his poems of the 1930s by his own confession of faith in his essay, "Purely Subjective," published in 1943:

> If a Christian is asked, "Why Jesus and not Socrates
> or Buddha or Confucius or Mahomet?" perhaps all
> he can say is "None of these arouse *all* sides of my
> being to cry, 'Crucify Him.'"

Still, this pronouncement of Auden's understanding of Christian selfhood seems remarkably harsh beside the graceful anticipation of Ultimate belonging that "He is the Way" proclaims. But in that contrast is a worthy theological idea: it is through the Cross that one reaches the resurrection.

Like Anselm of Canterbury in the eleventh century, Auden

understands the sacrifice of Jesus not as an event that satisfies God's mind. Rather this sacrifice satisfies God's expectation of unity or wholeness between God and creation, affording the fulfillment of the eternal blessedness for humanity that God had always intended, a blessedness thwarted by sin, brought again into new life by obedience even unto death on a Cross.

As in the Sermon on the Plain in Luke and the Sermon on the Mount in Matthew, the kingdom of God breaks into the present from the future. Perhaps for similar reasons Auden's hymn makes implicit comparison between the suffering and misery of the fallen human "city" on one hand, and Augustine's "City of God" on the other.

The Way, the Truth, and the Life do not provide escape from anxiety, nor platitudes for otherworldly expectation. The kingdom that breaks in upon us, that Christ would have us know, claim, and embrace is "in the World of the Flesh." Within his kingdom is resurrection: that "at your marriage all your occasions shall sing for joy."

—Louis Skipper

For another meditation based on this hymn, see AN INCONCEIVABLE INCARNATION, p. 42.

I Am Thinking

Meditation based on
"I am the bread of life," *Hymnal 1982*: 335

These are the thoughts I am thinking as I open my eyes one warm summer evening at Camp Wood. We are singing "I am the resurrection, I am the life. They who believe in me, even if they die, they shall live forever." I look around the circle at the beautiful, awkward, vital young people. Do they really know what they are singing? They know this song by rote. It was sung at this camp when my father went and every summer since. I stop and think about the words. They are kind of gross. Eating flesh, drinking blood. Do they understand communion? Do I? They still thirst and hunger. Do they know? Do they believe? "Yes, Lord, we believe that you are the Christ." Do they know what they are saying? But as they sing the chorus again, arms stretched up or around each other, I think perhaps they do know. They have the life within them.

These are the thoughts I am thinking as I open my eyes and look down at my flowers. The day has gone like a dream—better than any of my dreams of my wedding. As the people I love file past me on the way to the altar rail, I hear the familiar chorus: "And I will raise them up on the last day." What a glorious song! I begin to think about God. Jesus. This friend who has been with me through so much. High school heartbreaks, college when I drifted away, Africa when he was all I had, my parents' divorce—divorce, marriage. What have I just gotten myself into? I look over at my new husband and flirt. He laughs. I look up at my friends as they pass me and smile while singing.

Familiar. Friends. All this will be gone soon. I will step into another gaping unfamiliar. I will leave my family and friends today to begin a new life with this handsome gent in the tux sitting next to me. We will leave for a new town, new state, new friends, new school, new, new new. I am thinking: am I the same Kelly I was an hour ago?

I close my eyes and wrap this familiar song around me like my favorite flannel shirt.

—KELLY DEMO

Your Gift Is in My Giving, Lord

Your gift is in my giving, Lord;
my wealth I have from you.
Your love is in my loving, Lord,
when caring heart is true.

Your prayer is of my praying, Lord;
my heart must speak with you.
Your song is in my singing, Lord,
when praise shall rise anew.

My health is in your healing, Lord,
of all who turn to you.
My life is in your living, Lord,
when those three days were through.

Words: Mark D. Eddy
© 2005
Possible Tune: *Azmon*

When We Are Captives of Our Fears

When we are captives of our fears
and thrust into the boundless night,
refine our senses, God, to see
the refuge hidden by our fright.
Recall to us a holy place,
lit by the flame of Christ's pure light.

We trust that we are not alone
although in solitude we stand,
like your own son that dreadful night,
who asked his friends to stay at hand.
We seek the solace of our faith,
yet struggle as the gloom expands.

We listen to the night's soft sounds,
and breathe the scents of grasses green,
we feel the ground beneath our feet,
and trust your presence subtly seen.
God, permeate the world throughout
with Holy Spirit, love serene.

Words: Mary Ann Huston
© 2008
Possible Tune: *St. Petersburg*

My Grandmother's Garden

Meditation based on
"Morning has broken," *Hymnal 1982*: 8

I am unsure if my grandmother ever sang "Morning has broken." She and my grandfather attended a small nondenominational Christian church of the more fundamental variety. They sang the "good ol' hymns"—hymns that I was not familiar with having been brought up in the Episcopal Church. It is from going to church with her that I learned such songs as "Up from the grave he arose," "Higher ground," and "In the garden." As I said, I am unsure if my grandmother ever sang "Morning has broken," but nevertheless this is the hymn that I most associate with her and her life.

My grandmother was the closest person to a saint that I have ever known. In her I observed an almost Benedictine rule of life, long before I knew what Benedictine spirituality was. My grandmother lived out her faith on a daily basis. She had a rule of life (even if she never identified it as such) that focused her attention on God through the actions of her day-to-day existence. She raised four children, supported her husband who ran a business and was mayor three times, and was a matriarch of her church community. My grandmother was at church almost every time the door was opened. She cooked dinners for the community, served on their equivalent of an altar guild, attended Bible study, and, for most of her life, sang in the choir. In her old age, when she had become bedridden, I remember my grandmother still crocheting lap-robes for people who lived in the nearby nursing home.

Above all these things, however, I remember my grandmother most as a gardener.

She had a beautiful garden—it was in fact her whole yard. My mother and aunts used to say that my grandmother could make anything grow; "She has a green thumb," they would say. I believe this was true, as she always had clippings that were taking root in bottles in her kitchen window. She told me with great pride one time about one of the bushes in her yard that she had nurtured from a clipping that a friend of hers had pilfered from the grounds of Buckingham Palace.

Despite all of this success with her plants, my grandmother was under no illusion that her garden was due to her own personal prowess. In the middle of her backyard, she erected a sign that ascribed the glory of her garden to God. I later learned that this was a common garden sign, but for my grandmother it was truly a proclamation of faith: "One is nearer God's heart in a garden than anywhere else on earth." Even the sign she treated with reverence. I remember her applying a new coat of white enamel paint every few years and then hand painting the raised wrought iron letters of the prayer with black paint.

Blackbird has spoken, like the first bird

My grandmother was one of the few people I know who did not have air conditioning. When I spent the night, and especially in the spring and summer, we would sleep with the windows open. I remember hearing the first bird of the morning. And the sunlight filtering through the sheer curtains that blew on the breeze in her guest bedroom. After breakfast we would often work in the garden or visit the nursery to purchase some new plants.

Praise for the sweetness of the wet garden

My grandmother's backyard was laid out into two parts that were divided by a hedge. The portion of the yard closest to the house was the planned garden. Here beds of flowers were surrounded by patches of beautiful green grass. There were flower boxes and hanging baskets full of multicolor blooms. This formal garden was the area of the yard that my grandmother cultivated—the area that she planned and tended. Beyond the hedge lay the natural garden. Here there was no grass, and while there were some beds defined by natural rock borders, the plants that grew here were wildflowers and groundcovers. My grandmother shaped this section, but left it natural so that it could grow in its own pattern.

Sprung in completeness where his feet pass

It was only much later in my life that I realized the sacramental nature of Grandmother's garden. The section of the garden that she cultivated was an offering to God. She endeavored to fill this section with as much beauty as she could. When guests arrived, they were invited to sit in this section of the yard to visit amongst the beauty of the flowers. But this was not where my grandmother spent her private time in her garden. When she was alone, or when it was just the two of us, she retreated to the natural part of the backyard to sit in her swing and experience the beauty of nature as God created it without her help. This was her retreat. Here she would rest and contemplate and sing.

My grandmother's garden was a prayer—a very active form of prayer. There were moments of thanksgiving and moments of petition. These moments took place amidst the ordered beauty of her planned garden. And there were also moments of communion and contemplation. These moments took place in the solitude of the swing amongst dogwoods and ivy. These were the little moments when my grandmother taught me about being still in God.

Praise every morning, God's re-creation of the new day!

—Chad Vaughn

For another meditation on this hymn, see MORNING HAS BROKEN, p. 27.

At the Cross Her Vigil Keeping

Meditation based on
"At the cross her vigil keeping," *Hymnal 1982*: 159

When Maria held the babe in her arms, she knew she beheld a miracle from God. She and her husband, fifteen years her senior, had been incredulous at first upon hearing the unexpected news that she was pregnant. After the difficult birth of their daughter, the doctors had predicted that further pregnancies would be highly unlikely and probably life threatening. The resources available to this working class couple were limited and, as it was, their finances were stretched to the limit. Her faith was tested throughout this period of expectation, but never did her faith in her God succumb to her fears.

Now, here was the flesh of her flesh, love incarnate at her bosom. She knew this man child would be destined to do great things for his people. And so it was incomprehensible that this miracle child would be at death's door before his thirty-first birthday. Once more it was a time of trial for her. She learned to accept that AIDS was claiming the life of her beloved gay son. She learned to embrace all of who her son was, to rely on those who loved her son, and to confront those who despised her son. She accompanied him as he moved throughout the city with an air of bravura, defying AIDS to claim his spirit and joie de vivre. She shared in his elation when he received a hopeful medical prognosis. She witnessed his anger against a political and medical establishment that moved at a snail's pace to treat the poor, the gay men, the drug addicts, and the Haitian immigrants who suffered the first wave of this monstrous epidemic. She suffered his agony sometimes in silence, sometimes lamenting to Mary of Nazareth. Mary would understand a mother's sorrow at her son's suffering. Her faith at times was stretched to its limits, but never did her faith in God succumb to her despair.

I witnessed the last few moments of their life together. He had been having a terrible day, crying out in pain and she knew the end was near. It was breaking my own heart to see my brother suffer. I knew his cries were like a "sharp and piercing sword" tearing at our mother's heart. Her face was the last he saw as he made his transition into God's loving arms. When his body ceased to function with that last gasp of air, my tears began to flow, and my mother stopped me. "No," she said, "not yet. Let his spirit leave in peace, knowing that we loved him. These tears will delay his passage to heaven's gate." She made the final sacrifice, released her hold, and yielded his soul to God.

My mother's faith, while extraordinary, is not unique. This past summer, when I worked as a chaplain at Children's Hospital, I witnessed many faithful vigils like the one Mary had kept at the foot of the cross and Maria had kept at the foot of the bed. Señora Leticia had watched helplessly as her son suffered a brain aneurism that struck suddenly and viciously, leaving him in a vegetative state. She seemed so lonely and fragile at times.

I remember Señora Candida whose son had spent weeks in the intensive care unit with a variety of life-threatening ailments. She was always upbeat, with a funny anecdote to share, ready to confront a future fraught with such hospital visits.

I will never forget Mrs. Peres, who had to make the painful decision to stop any further chemo treatments and take her son home to die. For her there was no time for tears, as there were too few moments left with her precious child.

But what I remember most was their search for God in these incomprehensible moments and their trust in God's presence in their lives. Their faith at times was stretched so taut, like a violin string too tightly wound, that I feared it would snap and there would be no music, no lyric left to this song. Yet God was faithful as they had been and their faith survived their sorrow and their doubts.

These women are the spiritual descendants of women found in the Gospels of Matthew, Mark, Luke, and John. They are the daughters of Mary and of women such as Mary Magadalene; Mary the mother of James the younger and of Joses; Salome ("peace"); the mother of the sons of Zebedee; Joanna, the wife of Herod's steward Chuza; Susanna ("lily"); Jesus' mother Mary; her sister (Jesus' aunt); Mary, the wife of Clopas; and the women (many) who had followed him from Galilee. They are the unnamed women: the Syrophoenician woman, the hemorrhaging woman, and the woman who anointed Jesus at Bethany. They are the women who followed him, challenged him, fed him, stood at the foot of the cross and risked claiming his body. This woman's touch was with him from the beginning until the end.

Having known Jesus, the Word Incarnate, so intimately is perhaps what makes this hymn so poignant. As the lyricist writes:

Who upon that mother gazing,
in her trouble so amazing,
born of woman, would not weep?

Who of Christ's dear mother thinking,
while her Son that cup is drinking,
would not share her sorrow deep?

But if the hymn were simply about the sorrow and the tragedy, then why would anyone take their place by this mother's side? The lyricist asks and answers this question:

Near thy cross, O Christ, abiding,
grief and love my heart dividing,
I with her would take my place;
by thy guardian cross uphold me,
in thy dying, Christ, enfold me
with the deathless arms of grace.

It was the intimate, sacramental knowledge of the deathless arms of grace that brings new life into the world that gave the women in the Scriptures and in the hospital rooms the strength to be bowed but not broken. It is this intimate knowledge that propels many forward to continue living, loving, and struggling to heal a broken world.

Alla Renee Bozarth's poem, *Before Jesus,* vividly captures these women's wisdom and strength:

Before Jesus
was his mother.

Before supper
in the upper room,
breakfast in the barn.

Before the Passover Feast,
a feeding trough.
And here, the altar
of Earth, fair linens
of hay and seed.

Before his cry,
her cry.
Before his sweat
of blood,
her bleeding
and tears.
Before his offering,
hers.

Before the breaking
of bread and death,
the breaking of her
body in birth.
Before the offering
of the cup,
the offering of her
breast.

Before his blood
her blood.
And by her body and blood
alone, his body and blood
and whole human being.

The wise ones knelt
to hear the woman's word
in wonder.

Holding up her sacred child,
her God in the form of a babe,
she said: "Receive and let
your hearts be healed
and your lives be filled
with love, for
This is my body,
This is my blood."

Finally, I cannot help but wonder how Jesus' life story and ministry might have been written differently or the same if a woman had written an account?

—Maria Elizabeth (Liz) Muñoz

Text of poem from *Accidental Wisdom,* iUniverse 2003, and *This is My Body~Praying for Earth, Prayers from the Heart,* iUniverse 2004. Used by permission from the author.

I Came to Jesus

I came to Jesus torn within,
a sinking suffering soul.
I placed my care within his hands,
and now I am made whole.

Refrain:
Jesus, the name above all names,
your peace you freely give.
Whoever rests their faith in you,
will ever truly live.

I came to Jesus bruised and bare
of all that I had known.
He filled me with his boundless love,
and he has led me home.

O, come to Jesus as you are,
in need of sweet release.
Lay down your pain and sorrow there,
and he will grant you peace.

Words: Greg Garrett
© 2006
Possible Tune: *The Rowan Tree*

Lord, Let Your Servant Go in Peace

Metrical paraphrase of *Nunc dimittis*

Lord, let your servant go in peace;
your promise is fulfilled.
My eyes behold your chosen one,
whom you yourself have willed.

Your saving grace has been revealed
for all the world to see;
a light to lighten all the earth,
to set your people free.

Words: Jason Haddox
© 1999
Possible Tune: *St. James* or
This Endris Night

The Day Thou Gavest

Meditation based on
"The day thou gavest, Lord, is ended," *Hymnal 1982*: 24

The day thou gavest, Lord, is ended . . .

It took her just days to die, my friend. Well, weeks, really.
Months, if you count from the time the cancer returned with
a vengeance, insinuating its odious tentacles into every nook
and cranny, shutting down one organ at a time, till all that was
left was breath and hope. And then hope alone. And then a
sigh, and she was gone.

But days, it seemed to us; too few, too soon. Yet even as
she died, she gave us hope. Hope not just that the cancer might
be reversed. Hope that we might face our own deaths with
her grace and strength. And then the dying days. Days when
she could no longer speak. When death hovered just beyond,
waiting while we said our last good-bye, and good-bye, and I
love you; good-bye.

Often, when I believe the life before me must have slipped
away into another realm, when I think I am saying alone the
ancient words of our most familiar prayer, the silent lips begin
to move, to breathe with me, in a whisper only God can hear,
the words learned as a child. It is then that I hear afresh what
it is we pray: for the daily bread of strength and hope, for the
grace to forgive as we have been forgiven, for the vision to

perceive that God is listening. We speak our silent words, our love song to our God.

To thee our morning hymns ascended . . .

I have a book called *Bird Songs*: two hundred fifty varieties, from loon to grebe, in beautiful color prints. And bound into the cover is a device that reproduces the sound of each. Push the loon button and you're beside a starlit pond in Maine with the voice of a lonely bird telling his troubles to the moon.

Pity we haven't a bird button for this hymn, to carry its pure air from a distant choir. For sometimes, I believe, the melody is not just a vehicle for the text, interchangeable within its metrical setting. Sometimes the two are so interwoven, so mutually dependent, so truly wed in song and rhyme that they sing to God in perfect harmony. Then the hymn becomes not just a poem set to music. It is infused with a *logos* all its own in the voice of prayer and praise.

The lilting three-quarter time melody named *St. Clement* to which "The day thou gavest, Lord" is sung embodies that happy truth.

The hymn was written and set to music during the reign of Queen Victoria, the heyday of British colonialism, and was so beloved by Her Majesty that she asked that it be sung in churches throughout the realm in celebration of her Diamond Jubilee in 1897. It is not just a sweet evening lullaby, but a psalm of mission: it sings in tender tones of the stewardship of the British Crown and the Church of England over the far-flung dominions under their care. Ironically, a hundred years later, as the light of empire faded with the loss of Britain's colonies, this hymn was sung at the service handing over the governance of Hong Kong to the Peoples' Republic of China.

To dismiss it as a period piece, however, would be to lose

one of the most beautiful and elegiac of hymns. For it sings not only of the Church's never-sleeping ministry and mission in the metaphor of night and day, but of the alpha and omega of life itself. Small wonder that it is for many the funeral hymn of choice.

Thy praise shall sanctify our rest.

I have helped bury more than I can remember, and have learned too well how to live without the ones who made life worth living. I'm closing in on the age when the deaths of my generation are no longer tragic violations of the natural order, obscenely premature like the death of a child, but part of nature's rhythm, the slow concession of youth to age. The hour cometh, and now is, when I must own up to my own mortality, when the absolutely inconceivable must begin to give way to the inevitable.

It is in that awe-filled knowledge that I murmur John Henry Newman's beautiful prayer in the dark watches of the night: "O Lord, support us all the day long . . . until the shadows lengthen, and evening comes, and the busy world is hushed, and the fever of life is over, and our work is done. Then in thy mercy grant us a safe lodging, and a holy rest, and peace at the last."

Peace at the last: to the strains of *St. Clement*'s gentle waltz with God.

—ANNE KNIGHT HOEY

We Gather in This Holy Place

OFFERING
We gather in this holy place,
responding to your call,
united by amazing grace
and rescued from the fall.

THANKSGIVING
Praise be to you, blest One-in-three,
who draws us in with love.
We sing, we stand, we bend the knee,
and join the throng above.

BREAKING OF THE BREAD
Break bread, take cup, so we may live;
our sins are wiped away.
Our wills, our wealth, our breath we give
forever and today.

COMMUNION

As one we now draw near to you,
our life in you restored.
We take, we eat, we are renewed—
the body of our Lord.

Words: Sean Steele
© 2010
Possible Tune: *Land of Rest*
The four stanzas of this hymn relate
to the four parts of
The Holy Communion.

I Once Was There, When They Crucified My Lord

Meditation based on "Were you there when they crucified my Lord," *Hymnal 1982*: 172

The ragged men and women stumble in from their life out-doors, across a rickety front porch, carrying the stench of alcohol, homelessness, and cheap perfume. The body of wor-shippers gathers for a Holy Week service. Distrust keeps some of the guests distant and sitting alone. Others scan the room for those familiar faces that cook a meal, hold a service, and welcome them every Tuesday night. One doesn't have to go into detail for these guests at Guadalupe House to understand the suffering of Christ.

Swollen hands hold this evening's gospel reading with lit-tle stability but much desire. I've learned at Guadalupe House that heroin addicts' hands and feet swell up and turn red. It is a regular sight around our house. The reader, despite her trials outside our home, still offers her presence. Despite the demons of addiction and mental illness that she fights, she still offers to read the gospel for us. Most often she comes to us with stories of police abuse; authorities stalking and raping her. She usu-ally has elaborate escape plans—where she is going to move to once that next government check comes in the mail. Dreams and government checks seem to be lost in the heroin.

For us on this Tuesday evening it doesn't matter what has

really happened and what is delusion. It doesn't matter that she seems to be stuck in a cycle and using our home as a lifeboat in her sea of self-destruction. We gather every Tuesday to lift up both our suffering and joys, leaving all judgment aside.

Mara, a community member at Guadalupe House, leads the service. She passionately walks us through the days of Holy Week. At the end of the service, she closes us with song, standing in the middle of the room, surrounded by broken bodies on collapsed couches. Her voice rises about her, above us all. She shouts the sounds of a song we have all heard: "Were you there when they crucified my Lord?" The sound paralyzes the otherwise chaotic room. All are overtaken by the question of whether we were there. Were you present when Jesus—the one who brought good news that the last shall be first and the first last, the one who befriended questionable characters, the one who offered hope to an occupied people who desperately sought liberation from oppression—were you there to see that hope hung out to die?

Yes, we all have witnessed some of this passion, or else we would not be trembling ourselves. Mara's voice trembles with emotion. Hands fidget and tremble in anticipation of that next drink or fix. My throat trembles with the rise of emotion within me at the sight of God's body and blood broken for us in so many ways.

Emotion swells behind the sad eyes of an expectant and broken people gathered. Whether our suffering trails behind us in a stench, swells up our hands, or just eats us away inside, we are gathered as the broken body. We all ask ourselves the same question: Were we there when they crucified the Lord?

Looking around the room at all who have gathered to remember the suffering and look forward to the glory, I hear another song being sung:

Were you there when I lost my job?
Were you there when I found my friends were gone?
Were you there when they took away my kids?
Were you there when I gave up hope?
Were you there when the streets became my home?
Were you there when they raped me in the woods?
Were you there when I sold myself for dope?
Were you there when they committed me against my will?
Were you there when I tried to end my life?
Were you there when they numbed away my hope?
Were you there when they crucified my Lord?
Sometimes it causes me to tremble, tremble, tremble.

This song haunts me. I wonder if there will be a day when I am asked: Were you there when they crucified my Lord? Will I look future generations in the eye and tell them: No, I didn't know any suffering. No, I didn't know about my neighbor's struggle with addiction. No, I wasn't aware there were so many children dying from hunger.

I pray that I will be able to answer: Yes, I was there. All the suffering we needed to endure was done on the cross by Jesus Christ. But we go to the cross to remember this and find our strength to go out and care for the broken Body of Christ in the world.

I pray that our trembling in the face of suffering will be turned into radiant love to go out and heal, feed, and care for Christ among us now.

—JESSIE SMITH

Grace Has Kindled Our Desires

Grace has kindled our desires;
trusting, we shall be restored!
We renounce all evil powers,
follow and obey our Lord.
We believe in God the Father,
we believe in Christ the Son,
Death and Blessing in the water,
Holy Spirit, Three in One.

Holy Spirit, stir this water,
make this font a mighty sea.
Sink us in the crucifixion,
raise us in Christ's victory.
We believe in God the Father,
we believe in Christ the Son,
Joy and Suffering in the water,
Holy Spirit, Three in One.

Welcome to the holy household!
All adopted children we,
bathed in grace and marked as God's own,
facing Jesus, we are free.
We believe in God the Father,
we believe in Christ the Son,
Breath and Family in the water,
Holy Spirit, Three in One.

All disciples, in glad reverence
work to change and dare to heal,
bring God's kingdom to completeness,
each one loved, more fully real.
We believe in God the Father,
we believe in Christ the Son,
Fire and Singing in the water,
Holy Spirit, Three in One.

Words: Susanne D. Comer
© 2009
Possible Tune: *In Babilone*

He Is Alive

Somewhere the dark has to give;
somehow the light will shine through.
Sunlight is born from the earth:
it wakes us from sleep.
We wonder alone if
he is alive.

Opening doors we go out,
following paths we have trod.
Passing by strangers we stop,
our hands become one.
They wonder with us if
he is alive.
Is he alive?

Trembling we come to the tomb,
seeing the stone rolled away.
Searching, we warm in the sun
with tears in our eyes,
The stone, it cries out that
he is alive.
He is alive.

Wonder, the river of life
binds all our hearts into one.
Darkness has fled from our soul.
The Light is reborn.
Together we know that
he is alive,
he is alive,
we are alive,
he is alive.

Words: Austin K. Rios
© 2001

Easter Hymn for the Feast of St. Mary Magdalene

Sing out aloud my mounting Easter joy.
I saw the Christ in Eden just this morn.
He told me, "Mary, listen to my voice,
tell all my friends that now new life is born."

Fear not my sisters, brothers, Christ does live
and dwells in us when we do truly love.
Come, let us seek him and the gifts he'll give
on earth, our blessings fine as those above.

Put down your jar; leave all your nets behind.
The Lord calls us to go to Galilee.
Behold Christ's glory and God's grace, to find
good wine of Cana flowing fast and free.

Proclaim abroad the greatness of our God,
who has exalted Jesus to the skies.
We call him Wisdom, Teacher, Rabbi, Lord,
and in his spirit now so high we rise.

Words: Cynthia Briggs Kittredge
© 2008
Possible Tune: *Woodlands* or
Birmingham

He Is Risen

Meditation based on
"He is risen," *Hymnal 1982*: 180

> But the angel . . . said to the women,
> "Do not be afraid, for I know you seek Jesus who
> was crucified.
> He is not here; for He is risen."
> (Matt. 28:5–6, NKJV)

Life magazine chronicled the procession and burial of John F. Kennedy in poignant and indelibly vivid photographs. Yet in all these manifestations of the American good-bye, there was not one comparable to the tiny salute offered by three-year-old John. At the deepest level, that photograph tells us that it is not only the president who is dead, it is also his father. Truth goes beyond what can merely be seen. It goes beyond respect, honor, even the highest office in the land. The deepest truth comes from what is deeply felt, like a little boy who loves his dad.

The hymn "He is risen" is about this kind of truth— Easter truth—the kind of truth you can feel deeply. To over-romanticize this hymn and make it a sung creed or a religious "Pledge of Allegiance" is to crush its truth. We are not saluting the static risen Christ of twenty centuries ago, a Jesus frozen in first-century white linen like "Old Glory" shredded and encased in glass. No, the Easter truth is present tense: "He is risen." The Easter truth is personal and profound. It is owning our fragile mortality in a hope that there is more.

Behind Cecil Frances Alexander's acclamation that "He is risen" is the assertion that God's kingdom has come upon us. Christ has broken the bonds of death . . . *sin and pain can vex no more*. It is a truth not rooted in the intellect but in the heart, much like a three-year-old's salute. It is the affirmation that the risen Christ has ushered in a new age for us. He is the ever-present Lord.

Death's long shadows have departed . . . And I was standing within the first pew in the church of my baptism, encased in the presence of my mother, wife, brother, sister, and grandmother. The caskets were rolled down the aisle toward the front door and the awaiting black hearse. Enclosed in the caskets were my brother and his wife. We were singing "He is risen," but only some of the words came out. Through the tears clouding my eyes, I saw the two I loved ushered out by serious men in black suits.

And a brighter Easter beam on our longing eyes shall stream . . . The Easter truth is one of personal knowledge. It can only be examined or dissected in textbook or lecture, not known. The truth is better pronounced bursting forth from the sepulchre of the heart into the words of song: *He is risen. Tell it out with joyful voice.* In the midst of our greatest pain, the physical death of someone we dearly love, we cry out with these words, not as dogma, but as the hopeful truth implanted in us before the age.

He is risen . . . he has burst his three-day prison . . . And as the Coast Guard contingent came to stiff attention to honor my brother and his family, and the folded flag was handed to my mother, I, too, wanted to offer a solitary salute.

—Patrick Gahan

Lift High the Cross

Meditation based on
"Lift high the cross," *Hymnal 1982*: 473

Out of death and destruction arises life and resurrection. Amidst the rubble, new life emerges.

The cross is lifted high!

Picture in your mind the earthquake. That sudden moment, the groaning of the earth and the violent shaking. Then the loud cracking sound as buildings and homes begin to crumble. The screams . . . dust everywhere . . . darkness . . . the ground shaking . . . the roof falling in . . . utter darkness.

What went through your mind at that time? Can you remember? Were there cries for help? "O God, protect us!" "Most Holy God, save us!" Yes, even in the midst of the earthquake and all of the confusion that that entails, in the midst of the terror and fear, there was faith. And so you called out to the One by whose sign you were marked at baptism, "Blessed Jesus, help me!"

The earth stopped shaking. Just a few seconds ago there was chaos, people running for safety and screams heard all around. Now it is quiet. You look around to assess the situation. You are safe, holding tightly to loved ones—all trembling and crying. When you are finally able to talk, everyone does so all at once. You are all interested in how each of you had fared the crisis. Suddenly you realize how terrified and shaken you are. You are scared out of your wits! But at the realization that you're alive, there are shouts of praise. "Thanks be to God! I'm fine! Blessed be God! We're not harmed!"

The cross is lifted high!

You may be okay, but how about . . . ? Your mind races as you begin to imagine all sorts of situations and conditions in which you might find your loved ones and other friends and neighbors. Your mind is filled with names and faces, and immediately you begin to pray for them, "O God Almighty, please let them be alive and well. Most Holy Virgin, take care of them."

You're distracted by people's names being shouted everywhere. One name is heard above all others. God! God! GOD! Thanks be to God echoes throughout the streets. Thanks be to God echoes in the city. Thanks be to God echoes in the nation. Thanks be to God echoes in the world!

Later the family is together. You share the fear and sadness. You look about you and see so much destruction. Your valued possessions are all gone. The house your grandfather built is now a pile of rubble in the street. Only your kitchen remains. You begin to sift through what's left. Your eye catches sight of the image of the Sacred Heart of Jesus that hung on your bedroom wall. You pick it up and clutch it to your heart. The frame is broken and only fragments of glass remain. You think to yourself, "I'll reframe it." You hold it to your bosom, not wanting to let it go. It is so comforting. Some tears roll down your cheeks, as you ponder all that has happened. You don't know why and you decide that it is not meant for you to know.

God willed it to be this way. *Así lo quiso Dios.* And you move forward to put your life back together again.

Time moves on . . . the days pass. The memories are still there. You share your story with anyone who will listen. There is a mixture of emotions. Some people are angry with God for what took place. Others are simply thankful that God protected them. All, nonetheless, share the hope of the cross. Together you have shared the suffering of Christ; together you will share in Christ's redemption.

The community begins to see new life. The rubble is almost all gone. Homes and businesses are being rebuilt and new homes are being built. The streets are being widened. Many of you have indoor plumbing for the first time in your lives. And your old picture of the Sacred Heart in its new shiny frame is rehung on the wall. Hung with much love and devotion.

You have gathered together with family and friends who come to celebrate the Blessing of a New Home. What an exciting and joyful moment. You stand outside your new home, trying to take it all in. It is so beautiful. *¡Gracias a Dios! ¡Bendito sea el Señor!* You are so grateful and tears of joy stream down your cheeks as you recall life before the earthquake, remembering your old home and the memories shared there. Your former house is gone, but in its place stands your new abode where new memories will be made.

Do you remember, after the earthquake, after you had lost it all, thinking to yourself, "O my God, what will I do? How will I ever re-build? What is going to happen to me now?" In the midst of destruction, your faith sustained you as you looked to the future—praying and believing.

And now here you are, with your family and friends come to celebrate this moment with you, to give thanks to Almighty

God for your many blessings, to thank God for raising from the rubble and ashes this new creation, your new home.

Out of death and destruction, arises life and resurrection. Amidst the rubble, new life emerges.

The cross is lifted high!

At this moment you tell your story. You talk about the fear and sadness you felt. You share how your faith gave you hope to go on. How you encouraged others to go on, shouting the song of victory.

> *Lift high the cross,*
> *the love of Christ proclaim*
> *till all the world*
> *adore his sacred Name!*

—Anthony Guillen

Now the Green Blade Riseth

Meditation based on
"Now the green blade riseth," *Hymnal 1982*: 204

It is an annual event. No, more than an event, it is a part of the fabric of our lives. In the dead of winter, nothing green can be found anywhere; but we know that lying just beneath the ground are small pieces of grain, seeds, seemingly lifeless, that will soon shoot forth from the darkness of the earth with life-filled color. All at the same time, it seems. Now the green blade riseth. This is the presence of God, showing love for us—that out of death can be brought life, out of the dead grain can be brought a new living plant.

This is the love of God: that in what seemed the darkest, deepest winter of the history of humankind, love could spring forth. Jesus, the Word, the Logos, lay dead. People thought they were rid of him forever, that when he was put in the tomb they could get on with their plans. But this is the love of God: that even in death there is infinite potential for life. That when something is buried, it can always, in some way, give life. This is part of the fabric of our lives. It is more than an event; we must come to expect it regularly. We *can* expect it regularly.

Easter, the spring of the year when everything shoots forth from the earth! What a perfect time to celebrate Christ, risen from the dead! I remember as a child loading up a mite box with flowers to take to church for the flowering of the cross. The processional hymn would always be "Jesus Christ is risen today," accompanied by trumpets. Everyone would have on new clothes, and it would take forever to receive communion. After church we would always go to my grandmother's house for a big lunch, and then sit around afterward for a long time, just talking. But what does this really have to do with the love of God, given to us in the death and rising of Jesus Christ? It has everything to do with this, because it is part of the fabric of our lives. We know God where we see love.

There are many who don't have such memories of Easter. There are many who have not experienced the love of God. There are many whose hearts are dead to the love that God has given to us in the death and rising of Christ. There are many whose lives are wintry, constantly full of grief and pain. They look over the field of their heart and all they see is barrenness, darkness, and no signs of life at all. But even in these hearts there lie seeds from which life can spring. Even in these hearts, God can touch the death there and bring forth life.

How does this happen? How does the green blade rise out of this death? This is the love of God, that seeds are scattered from one field to another. The wind blows seeds and grain from field to field. From heart to heart the love of God is sowed. Only when the green blade rises and grows in us can it be spread to others. This is how the gift of God can grow from season to season, from year to year, from Easter to Easter. It must be a part of the fabric of our lives.

—PATRICK J. WINGO

Singing in the Cave Monastery

Meditation based on "For all the saints
who from their labors rest," *Hymnal 1982*: 287

I sat in the lobby of Methodist Hospital in Houston recently, a marble atrium lobby complete with fountain. It looked exactly like the lobby of an exclusive hotel, and I thought about being in the center of one of the world's most advanced medical complexes, and yet the mortality rate for life is still 100 percent.

I thought of dying patients I saw during the summer's chaplaincy work and the patients I knew in my previous nursing career. I thought of the grieving families I've dealt with, and the tragedies of lives ended suddenly in suffering. I thought of the infant I baptized this summer who died, who never saw the light of day, and the man who died of AIDS nine days after he was diagnosed, and the eighty-five-year-old lady who died with her husband of sixty-five years holding her hand. And I remembered others I've known who've died. My dear grandmother who taught me her favorite Psalm—"I will lift up mine eyes unto the hills, from whence cometh my help." And I remembered my playmate when I was ten who was killed in a sledding accident. And I thought of my father who died six years ago in a bedroom of our home. He'd taught me the Lord's Prayer and read my Sunday school lessons to me before I learned to read. And I remembered the song I sang on the day of my father's funeral—

"For all the saints." That hymn "worked" for me on his funeral day because it is a song of hope about the resurrection life of all the saints. And the hymn "works" for me in remembering the patients I've seen die and the families and friends who've grieved.

Many people, Christians included, live their lives in fear of death. And yet in our baptismal covenant we have the promises of God about our present and future communion with all the saints. This covenant is our affirmation of what God has promised and done for us by his grace. And this covenant is our testimony, our witness and confession of God's action and involvement in the world.

But this confession, this witness, is not easy. Paul called his disciple Timothy to a fight of faith. He said, "Fight the good fight of the faith; take hold of the eternal life, to which you were called and for which you made the good confession" (1 Tim. 6:12). It's not easy to live in a world that denies faith in a resurrection life. "O may thy soldiers, faithful, true, and bold, fight as the saints who nobly fought of old. . . . We feebly struggle, they in glory shine; yet all are one in thee, for all are thine."

The faith of the saints "who nobly fought of old" and our continued fellowship with them was never more clearly experienced than during my visit to the Soviet Union in the summer of 1988. I especially remember our visit to the Cave Monastery in Kiev. The caves of the monastery are a tourist attraction because the monks of seven and eight centuries ago have been mummified by the natural conditions of the cave and are displayed in shrouds and open caskets. So we lined up with all the Soviet tourists and wondered what monks who had died seven hundred years ago would look like. With our lighted tapers bought for one kopeck a piece, we followed narrow stone corridors down into the earth. There—in the niches in the walls and some in small rooms that had served as cells where monks had lived—were tiny open sarcophagi containing shrouded figures. There was a sense of wonder at seeing the physical remains of Christians who had lived there so long ago and served God in their strange calling in the caves. They were reminders of the sustaining presence of God in deep and sometimes hidden ways over the centuries while governments change and persecute.

I don't know who started it, but spontaneously our group began to sing, "For all the saints, who from their labors rest, who thee by faith before the world confessed, thy Name, O Jesus, be forever blessed. Alleluia, Alleluia!" Our singing filled the caves and echoed outside through the hills of the monastery. It was one of those wonderful moments of pure worship of God and joyous expression of thanksgiving for our heritage through the saints.

As our group left the caves and went into the courtyard, the abbot found us and wanted to know who we were and what we'd been singing. A crowd of Soviets surrounded our group and through our guides we explained who we were. After telling us about the recent return of the monastery from the government, and the persecution he had experienced, the abbot asked us to sing again the hymn we'd sung in the caves. Our guide translated it first for him, and then we sang it again for the unexpected audience of a Russian Orthodox monk and a crowd of Soviet citizens.

The language differences and the distance of centuries and thousands of miles fell as silenced barriers in our witness of the communion of saints. The sense of unity with monks who lived seven centuries ago and a Russian abbot and a crowd of Americans and Soviets was a proleptic experience of the promise of eternity in one moment of singing perfect "Alleluias!"

—MARY GREEN

We Know That Christ Is Raised and Dies No More

Meditation based on "We know that Christ is raised and dies no more," *Hymnal 1982: 296*

You are in your car and a song comes on the radio. As you listen to the music, you are transported back to the eighties. The song reminds you of your first dance, your first kiss, your first love. It is as if some kind of musical déjà vu happens, and you find that your muscles, mind, and heart are experiencing that wonderful first kiss all over again. After a few seconds, you regain your thoughts, recognize that the light is now green, and blush over the highly embarrassing fact that the song that has affected you so greatly is by REO Speedwagon or Air Supply.

Music is powerful. Not only does it move you in the present moment with its beautiful melodies and image-invoking words, but it also has the potential to move you through time. You hear a melody and all of the sudden you are remembering something special, something from your past. You know what I am talking about. I am sure many, if not most of us, have been taken aback or taken back in time by music.

Some songs can move us to the brink of tears if not full-blown sobs—yes, even songs in church. There are many reasons to shed tears, just as there are many hymns that move us to tears. Some hymns we simply can bear no longer. If you are a youth minister, "Shine, Jesus, shine" sends you over the edge.

Those who minister to children have shed many a tear over "I sing a song of the saints of God." If you are a huge "Mr. Bean" fan, you can't quite make it through "All creatures of our God and King" without laughing so hard that you end up crying.

Or maybe, just maybe, the hymns you have sung time and time again in church conjure up special times, special memories, special moments between you and God. It gives us an opportunity to articulate, albeit for a brief moment, our trust in God and our desire to participate with God in reconciling his beloved people to him.

At baptisms, when we start to sing "We know that Christ is raised and dies no more," I have to bite my lip and take a deep, deep breath. I imagine that big, deep breath lets the Spirit into your heart and cultivates space in order for you to remember your baptism.

The Christian life begins with baptism. And throughout our Christian life we learn and live out that Christ is raised and dies no more. It is through our baptism that we become living members of the church, the Body of Christ. We are a new creation in Christ, invited, encouraged, and challenged to actively grow, transform, and live out our Christian lives working with and for God in order to share with all people God's plan of restoration.

Living an Easter life—that is joyous enough. Why cry? This hymn remembers us into Christ's body time and time again. It reminds us of who we really are and to whom we really belong.

I did not have the privilege of being baptized as an infant. I did not grow up in a Christian household and I dare to say, growing up I did not know God. I know what it is like to not be part of the Body of Christ. I grew up not knowing what Alleluia meant, and I clearly and vividly remember a time without knowing God.

Living without God is like treading water—it is an endless exercise in staying afloat. In order to stay afloat, you have to fend for yourself; it is too risky to let someone else tread water with you. They might hinder your success, or worse, you might have to help them. You are physically and emotionally exhausted from the constant movement of your body and mind. All you want is for someone, anyone, to throw you a life preserver or at least help you swim.

In our baptism we are invited to stop treading water. In our baptism, we are invited to jump into the water and die with Christ. Through our baptism, we plunge into the Christian life. We come out of the waters of baptism, having died to our former selves, and we are indeed a whole new creation. We come out intimately connected to the Body of Christ. We are joined into a communion of believers and we are invited and privileged to participate in the Body's efforts to restore the whole universe to God and teach humanity exactly what Alleluia means.

This beautiful baptismal hymn assumes much. It assumes we know that Christ is raised and dies no more. It assumes we share by water in his saving death. It assumes we live with God the Three in One. And it assumes the universe restored and whole will sing!

Let us not assume that the tears that come to us when we sing are sentimental folly or our weariness showing. Instead, let us assume that this movement of our souls could possibly be the Spirit helping us to become impassioned Christians responding in faith to our baptismal promises. So go ahead, no matter what the hymn—bite your lip, and take a deep, deep breath. Let the Spirit into your heart, and remember your special moments in community, your special moments with God.

—BETH WYNDHAM

People of God

People of God,
gather together,
come, let us sing on this glorious day.
Shouting abroad
praise to the Maker,
come and with body and soul let us pray.

Refrain:
Come, let us join in the heavenly dance,
praising in joyous celebration.

Hearing God's word,
heeding the message,
come and rejoice as we answer the call.
With one accord,
made in God's image,
come in community, welcoming all.

Bearing your gifts,
enter God's presence;
come, let us share in the heavenly feast.
Mending all rifts,
healing divisions,
come and from sorrows and hurts be released.

Women and men,
harmony blending,
come, swell the chorus in loving accord.
Raising again
thanks never ending,
come to the God who is Wisdom and Word.

Words: Patricia Blaze Clark
© 2003 Selah Publishing,
www.selahpub.com
All rights reserved.
Used by permission.
Possible Tune: *Earth and all stars*

This hymn, in its present form, was written for the fiftieth anniversary of the founding of the Seminary of the Southwest.

Index of Topics and Keywords

Index of First Lines:
Student-Written Hymns

Index of Meditations
by Hymn Title

Index of Authors